REIKi
Usui & Tibetan

LEVEL I
Certification Manual

Energy Healing for Beginners

By
GAIL THACKRAY

Printed in the United States of America
REIKI, Usui & Tibetan LEVEL I, Certification Manual, *Energy Healing for Beginners*
Thackray, Gail

ISBN-10: 0984844031
ISBN-13: 978-0-9848440-3-6

Project Editor, Mara Krausz
Illustrations by Rachel Harris
Layout and design by Teagarden Designs

Published by
Indian Springs Publishing
P.O. Box 286
La Cañada, CA 91012
www.indianspringspublishing.com

With special thanks to my Reiki Master and Teacher

Pauline Landy
My lovely aunt to whom I not only owe my Reiki lineage,
but the one responsible for putting me on my spiritual path
and encouraging me to teach.

CONTENTS

CHAPTER 1
WHAT IS REIKI?

Welcome to Reiki. Reiki (pronounced Ray-Key) is an energy transfer, a "hands-on" healing technique that is probably thousands of years old.

Reiki is a very simple form of healing that anyone can learn but creates extremely powerful results.

It is independent of religion and should not compete or detract from any religious practices.

This is a beautiful and powerful natural healing system. At the beginning level, this involves placing your hands slightly above your recipient and directing healing energy. At more advanced levels, it can be used to direct energy to people at a distance and to events in the past and the future.

Reiki – Rei means "Universal" and Ki means "Life Force"

When people talk about Reiki, they could be talking about two things: either the system of Reiki healing or the Reiki energy itself.

The system of Reiki is the natural healing modality that we are going to be learning. It involves working with a connection to Spirit and white light energy from God, or a higher being, to bring physical and emotional healing to the recipient. This is an ancient healing art that was possibly practiced in ancient Egypt and, even before that, in Atlantis and Lemuria. Dr. Usui, considered the founder of modern Reiki, harnessed this healing modality into a system of symbols and hand positions in Japan in 1922. This is the most widely practiced branch of Reiki – the Usui Ryoho system. Although Reiki appears to have been practiced in other areas of the East, such as Tibet. We are going to be learning about the Usui system and also incorporating the Tibetan Reiki traditions.

The energy of Reiki is often what someone refers to when they say the word "Reiki." Reiki energy is the Chi or life force energy that runs through each of us and is directed and transferred during a Reiki session.

The word Reiki comes from the words Rei and Ki put together.

> **Rei** – The general definition or translation of this word is "**Universal.**" However, the Japanese characters of the word actually contain several levels and can be more completely translated to mean "Spiritual Consciousness" or the consciousness of one's Higher Self or God. Such Spiritual Consciousness is all-knowing and guiding. Therefore, the Rei is the understanding or guiding of the energy that is directed in the perfect way to heal whatever is needed.

> **Ki** – Is translated as "**Life Force**" and is the same as the word "Chi" in many other cultures. This is the non-physical energy that flows through all living things. This vital force connects and pervades us all. This is our life energy. This is Divine Source or God energy.

Therefore Reiki, the word combining **Rei** and **Ki**, means "**Universal Life Force**" or the directing or channeling of Chi energy to the right place for the healing that is needed or asked for.

The Natural Flow of Ki

We are all part of an energy grid or energy field where Ki (Chi) energy flows through our physical bodies, between us, and in the space surrounding us. This energy field that we live in defines how energy flows to us and away from us. Our physical world is made up of particles of matter, atoms and molecules that are constantly vibrating and in motion. Even objects that appear to be solid are actually trillions of atoms which are not solid at all, but matter in motion. Even where we cannot see matter, we are still surrounded by an energy field. Flowing through this energy field is invisible chi energy or Reiki energy.

Sometimes without knowing it or without being tuned to Reiki specifically, we are still using and directing this energy. This is the energy that manifests physical things or experiences into our existence. This is the energy directed by prayer or positive thinking.

> Reiki energy is the Chi or life force energy that runs through each of us and is directed and transferred during a Reiki session.

Some Reiki Masters will tell you that Reiki is a special type of energy that is not readily available to all but rather something that you can only gain through Reiki attunements. It is my belief that this energy is already all around us but that Reiki attunements give us a special channel or connection to the spirit world to enhance and direct this energy, thus magnifying its strength many times over and directing it in a specific manner for healing, protection, and wellbeing.

It is a bit like learning a foreign language. When we visit a foreign country, we can still communicate our basic needs to people without being able to speak the language, but we can connect more easily and clearly when we can speak it. Here we are learning the language of communication for this spiritual lineage.

Reiki Channeling

Reiki channeling is the specific channeling of the Reiki energy. Once a person has been given an "attunement" or an initiation to this energy, they become a channel and can work with Spirit to direct this energy.

Reiki Has Intelligence

Reiki has its own intelligence. A Reiki channel can direct the energy but the energy will also go where it is needed.

What Reiki Feels Like

Both the recipient and the sender may feel the effects of Reiki. Some people feel an increased warmth and/or a tingly or electric sensation. Some may feel like fingertips are touching them (even if the sender's hands are not placed in that area). Most feel a deep relaxation and sometimes a recipient will even fall asleep.

Reiki Heals the Sender

Reiki aids the sender. A Reiki healer receives this energy which is used in their own body before aiding the recipient.

Psychic Reiki or Mainstream Reiki

The practice of Reiki healing has become widespread, now being offered in some hospitals, doctor's offices, and it is sometimes even covered by insurance. Becoming a Reiki healer involves an attunement to energies in spirit and then working with a connection to the other side, using the help of guides in spirit and Universal light energy. However, more mainstream teachings place the emphasis on the system of hand positions, symbols, and being a channel to the healing energy. Reiki Masters who come from a more spiritual slant often put the emphasis on the connection to Spirit, intuition, and being guided by Spirit. There is less emphasis on the hand positions with this approach. As a medium, you can probably guess which camp I'm in. I like to teach my students to develop a connection with their guides in spirit and to feel and experience the spiritual aspects, allowing themselves to be guided by the spirits who perform the healing.

No matter whom you learn from or who attunes you, one thing is for sure. Making the decision to become a Reiki Healer and open your heart to Reiki energy will change your life forever.

> Reiki aids the sender. A Reiki healer receives this energy which is used in their own body before aiding the recipient.

CHAPTER 2

A REIKI RESOLUTION

Healing is not only physical, it is a change of our higher being. We need to affirm our ideals and live in responsibility with more respect for others. By living in responsibility, you are taking charge of your own health. It is the understanding that what you are, is simply a reflection of your own thoughts, and your health is a reflection of your past state of mind, which can be changed. By living in responsibility, you are aware of your surroundings and that the way you live your life affects others, as well as Mother Earth and even generations to come.

REIKI IDEALS

Just for today, I will let go of anger

Just for today, I will let go of worry

Just for today, I will give thanks for my many blessings

Just for today, I will do my work honestly

Just for today, I will be kind to my neighbor and every living thing

— By the founder of Usui Reiki Ryoho, Dr. Usui

As Dr. Usui relates, we need to live in the NOW. Start by being responsible for yourself, today.

As we make an agreement with our guides that they will work through us and provide Reiki energy, we are also agreeing to develop our own sensibility and respect others, becoming a more understanding, balanced, and harmonious person.

CHAPTER 3

WHAT IS REIKI USED FOR

Reiki uses and effects:

- Physical healing
- Emotional healing
- Spiritual healing
- Healing past life issues
- Removing the cause of the illness, not just the symptoms
- Releases stress and anxiety
- Balances energy and chakras

- Increases physical energy
- Enhances spiritual growth
- Expands creativity
- Increases positive manifesting
- Connection to Divine Source
- Develop a more positive attitude

Reiki healing occurs at the source of the issue. If Reiki is directed at a physical ailment such as cancer, the Reiki will heal the cause of the cancer. Reiki will go back to the karmic and past life issues as well as the emotional issues in this life that are the actual root cause of the issue. So when a physical healing takes place, a deeper spiritual healing has taken place as well.

Reiki is not only about physical healing, but Reiki opens up a deep connection inside of you. Becoming a Reiki channel gives you a stronger connection to Source that brings with it, a higher understanding, clearer intuition, and a complete opening of your psychic senses. As you use this wonderful energy, all areas of your life will open up as a result of having a closer guidance system in your life and being more in tune with your "intuition."

I feel on my life's path when I help others connect to Divine Source.

When you receive and channel Reiki energy, your chakras are kept open and clean, giving you energy and vitality. When our energy is balanced and our chakras are working in harmony, our life works harmoniously.

Having become a Reiki channel, life will have a higher purpose and meaning as you feel like you are on your soul purpose. You will find that your life becomes more joyful and abundant, as you are able to resolve your own life lessons more quickly. Opening up to Reiki creates a stronger connection to the spirit world and your intuition, resulting in a greater ability to manifest positive things into your life.

Chapter 4
REIKI OPENED MY WORLD

I believe that it doesn't really matter whether we start our spiritual development through Reiki, mediumship, animal communication, prayer, meditation, or through another method. We are working on our spiritual connection: our connection to Source, to the other side, to God, and opening ourselves to receiving Divine guidance. The guidance that we feel comes from our guides, spirits, and angels that are with us on our journey.

Personally, my spiritual connection started with Reiki. Being introduced to this wonderful Reiki energy by my Auntie Pauline was the launch of my spiritual development. It is the spotlight that opened up my being and its impact would place me on my life's purpose. I believe that Reiki not only allowed wonderful healing energies to channel through me but opened me up spiritually in many ways. It allowed me to communicate as a medium with spirits on the other side, as well as with animals and other beings. More importantly, it made me much more aware of the world that I live in and the role that I play. My life has absolutely become more abundant and joyful since I have been opened to the Reiki energy.

Reiki attunements open up an eighth chakra. This chakra is about 6-8 inches above and two inches forward from the Crown Chakra on your spiritual body. This chakra is your connection to the Divine Source. It is called an Alpha Chakra. With your Level I Reiki attunement, this chakra starts to appear, and as you receive your level II through Master attunements, this chakra gets stronger and stronger.

My Story

I had come to the U.S. to pursue a career of a more business, down-to-earth nature. Meanwhile, back in England, my Auntie Pauline had undergone a major life change and after years of study, became a Reiki Master. While visiting me in California, she taught me the art of Reiki. When she did my level I attunement, she told me that this would open up a whole new realm to me and that things may start appearing.

Shortly afterwards, I attended a weekend seminar with a renowned British psychic. Something amazing happened to me that weekend. I found that in a room of complete strangers, I was able to pass on detailed messages from their loved ones in spirit. It was as if this ability had been there all along, that these spirits were just waiting outside, looking in patiently through the window. When I opened that door and said, "Come on in and talk to me," I had spirits lined up ready to chat, as clear as if I were standing next to you. It was then that I launched my career as a psychic medium.

> Being attuned to Reiki was about to open up a whole new world.

Sometime after that and just by coincidence (as if there were such a thing), I was at a crystal shop where an animal communicator was giving a workshop. Curious, I decided to attend and to my surprise, I found that animals came through to me just as easily as spirits and in exactly the same way! As my Auntie had told me, being attuned to Reiki was about to open up a whole new world.

My mission is to bring Reiki energy to as many as I can. I feel on my life's path when I help others open and connect to Divine Source. For me, initiation into Reiki is one of the keys to opening and connecting with the other side.

CHAPTER 5

BRIEF HISTORY OF REIKI

Reiki is an ancient form of healing thought to date back to our earliest civilizations. Both Tibetan and Usui Reiki symbols have been found in ancient Egypt and other parts of the world. Reiki was rediscovered and put into a formal system in Japan by Mikao Usui, more commonly known as Dr. Usui. Dr. Usui's work forms the basis of much of our Western Reiki teachings. Reiki was also practiced in Tibet. Although some of the symbols are different, much of the practice is the same. The teachings in this manual apply to both the Usui and Tibetan practice of Reiki. Only at the higher levels will you learn symbols and traditions that differ.

USUI REIKI

Dr. Usui was a Buddhist who devoted his life to the healing arts. He found that most healing systems left the practitioner feeling drained after giving a treatment. He hoped to find a better way to heal people without being depleted of energy afterward. Dr. Usui traveled the world for many years searching. During his journey, he learned Sanskrit in order to read ancient Buddhist texts that would aid him in his quest.

It was in 1922 that Dr. Usui did a 21-day retreat on Mt. Kurama, a sacred mountain in Japan, where he fasted, meditated, and prayed. It was on the last day that he received the Reiki energy. Since the story of Reiki is mostly passed down by word of mouth, there are several variations of this story and the complete facts may never be known.

Dr. Usui's 21-Day Fast

During Dr. Usui's retreat on Mt. Kurama, he collected 21 stones, and each morning he would throw out a stone to count the number of days. Every day he sat and meditated, hoping to receive insights. On the 21st morning, as the sun rose, he still had not received the insights that he had hoped for. On this last morning he was meditating underneath an overhang where water drops were hitting his Third Eye. As he sat in meditation, he watched the sun rising up over the horizon. Then he knew something

Mikao Usui

was unusual. It was if the sun were a ball of light coming right at his Third Eye. He was a little unsure but knew he should just allow this. As the ball of light hit his Third Eye, Dr. Usui saw symbols. He recognized these symbols, probably from a past life, but did not know their meaning. Then other balls came with other symbols. Dr. Usui was actually being attuned by Spirit, and the symbols he saw were ancient Reiki symbols.

As Dr. Usui came around from this unusual meditation, he thought it had lasted for maybe ten minutes. However, the sun was now directly above him in the sky. He must have lost track of time. He realized he must have been in this deep meditation for about six hours!

The Legend of the Four Miracles

He knew something very special had occurred, but he didn't know what this all meant.

Then he experienced what has become known as the "Four Miracles." As he started back down the mountain, he stubbed his toe on a rock. It was bleeding badly and when he instinctively placed his hand over the toe, it stopped bleeding. This was the first miracle. Then when he arrived down the mountain, he became very hungry. He went to a nearby restaurant and ate a large meal. After a fast such a large meal should have caused him indigestion but he was fine. (the second miracle). The girl who served him complained of a toothache. Dr. Usui placed his hands on her jaw and the toothache immediately disappeared (the third miracle). When Dr. Usui arrived back at the monastery, one of the older monks lay in bed with severe arthritis. Dr. Usui placed his hands on the monk. Immediately he felt better (the fourth miracle).

Healing the Poor

Dr. Usui knew then that he had been blessed with great healing energy. He wanted to use this incredible energy to heal as many people as possible. He began with those whom he thought needed it the most. These were the poorest people in town, the beggars around Kyoto. He did this work selflessly for many years, not accepting money for healing -and helping those most disadvantaged. Then one day he saw a man begging that he had healed sometime before. The man complained that he didn't want to be healed

Dr. Chujiro Hayashi

and preferred to be a beggar. He said it was easier than working for a living. It was then that Dr. Usui realized not everyone wants to be healed. This realization was a major turning point. After this, Dr. Usui decided to work on people that came to him seeking a healing, rather than the poor he thought needed it. Dr. Usui also decided to teach others to heal themselves.

The Spread of Reiki to the West

Dr. Chujiro Hayashi, a retired medical officer in the Japanese Navy, began studying with Dr. Usui in 1925. Dr. Usui gave his blessing to Dr. Hayashi to open his own healing clinic and to expand and continue the teachings of Reiki, which he did after Dr. Usui's passing from a stroke on March 9th, 1926.

Mrs. Hawayo Takata was of Japanese descent but living in Hawaii. She was in Japan for a family matter and went to the hospital for severe abdominal pain, a tumor, and a lung condition. The doctors told her that she was in need of surgery but wanting a non-surgical alternative, she was referred to Dr. Hayashi's clinic. Mrs. Takata was completely healed by Reiki and under Dr. Hayashi's tutelage, she became a Reiki Master in 1938.

Mrs. Takata opened several clinics in Hawaii and taught Reiki as well. She taught students up to level II. In 1970, she began to attune Reiki Masters and initiated twenty-two Masters before she died in 1980. These Masters then taught others, and so it was through Mrs. Takata that Reiki began to spread through the West.

Alternate Story

An alternate story that was told in much of the West is that Dr. Usui was brought up as a Christian who learned some Buddhist teachings. The story goes that Dr. Usui attended university in America and was teaching bible studies in Japan when a young boy asked that if Jesus could heal then why couldn't others. This started Dr. Usui's quest for a healing modality.

> The energy goes back to Atlantean and Lemurian times. It is not only ancient but universal and may not even be limited to this planet.

It appears that this twist to the history was created to help Westerners to be more open to studying Reiki. Research has shown that there is no factual basis to this story. There is also no evidence that Dr. Usui was a medical doctor. It is presumed that the prefix "Dr." was given to him either in relevance to his work as a Reiki healer or to show that he was a professional man of standing in society.

Origins of Reiki

So where did the original Reiki energy come from and who developed the sacred Reiki symbols that Dr. Usui received as an attunement from spirit? This remains a mystery. Similar sacred symbols have been found in Egyptian history and many other ancient cultures. However, it is thought that the energy goes back to Atlantean and Lemurian times. It is not only ancient but universal and may not even be limited to this planet.

Mrs. Hawayo Takata

Reiki Lineage

A Reiki healer today can be taught the hand positions and symbols, but they must be indoctrinated to receive these energies from a Reiki Master who attunes them so they become a channel to the energy. Each Usui Reiki Master can trace back his lineage to Dr. Usui.

Secret Reiki

Although there is now evidence that both Dr. Usui and Dr. Hayashi gave written materials to their students, Reiki was taught by subsequent teachers in great secrecy for many years. As a student learned the symbols, all materials would be destroyed as only a Reiki Master could pass on the sacred symbols. Because of this former practice of oral teaching, there are now many small variations in the Reiki teachings.

Affordability of Reiki

In Japan, Reiki was considered a revered sacred system and in order to learn it, one would have to show a great commitment of both time and energy. When Mrs. Takata first brought Reiki to the West, she wanted to impart the seriousness and value of this. To accomplish this in a way that Westerners could relate to, she charged $10,000 to become a Reiki Master. This ensured that the student was very serious about learning, but it made it cost prohibitive for most aspirants. Eventually, learning Reiki became affordable and because of this, it has spread rapidly. There are now thousands of Reiki Masters around the world. The word of Reiki has spread and the opportunity is now there for all who wish to receive this energy and to become practitioners themselves.

CHAPTER 6

LEVELS OF REIKI

In the Usui system, there are four levels. Although some teachers combine Level III/Advanced and the Master for a total of three levels. In my training, I use the Tibetan Reiki symbols in addition to the traditional Usui symbols and attune my students to both symbols, as well as teach them how to use them.

At **Reiki Level I** you receive an attunement and learn how to use the Reiki energy for hands-on sessions, both to heal yourself and others. It opens up the channels in the body for Reiki to flow, connecting you to Divine Source at a higher level than that attained through just meditation. Once attuned, you are always attuned.

At **Reiki Level II** you receive three of the sacred symbols and additional attunements that allow you to perform Reiki at a distance, and also into the future and the past. At Level II you learn to use your intuition more, beginning to be guided by your Reiki guides and Masters in spirit and to feel direction from Divine Source. Level II Reiki provides a higher vibrational energy and a stronger Reiki connection, bringing increased sensitivity and intuitive awareness.

At **Advanced Reiki Training (ART)/Level III** you receive advanced Reiki training and tools. At this level you receive the fourth of the four sacred Usui symbols, the Usui Master Symbol, and an attunement to this energy. You will also be given additional tools in Reiki and beyond that you can use while following your Reiki guides in giving your sessions. You will be listening to and be directed by your Reiki guides and Masters. At this stage, further change is inevitable and the individual will be well aware of this fact from the changes that will have occurred already.

At the Master Level you receive the Tibetan Master symbol and the breath training that will give you the ability to pass attunements to others. This gives you the ability to teach and pass Reiki to others. You will learn how to give self-attunements, psychic attunements, and healing attunements. It is important to be clear that initiation into the Master degree in Reiki does not turn anyone into an enlightened Spiritual Master, but rather to a Master of their own self and a commitment to undertake and evolve to this state.

CHAPTER 7

REIKI GUIDES

SPIRIT GUIDES, REIKI GUIDES, AND ANGELS

We are all born with a main spirit guide that is assigned to us at birth and stays with us throughout our life. We also have a Guardian Angel. When you are attuned to Reiki, you are being attuned to other guides in spirit. These are guides and Masters that vibrate with the Reiki energy and wish to work with you for healing. They could be people who lived on earth and practiced Reiki, or they could be other entities that wish to work with this specific system. You will probably be working with many different spirits in your Reiki healing, though some may come more often to you than others.

> Be open to receiving the spirits from the white light that wish to work with you and the most appropriate ones for each healing will come.

You may also call in angels that wish to work with the Reiki energy. Perhaps you wish to call in Archangel Raphael, who is known for healing, or other spirits that you have around you. Do not think that you only have one Reiki Master that looks like an Asian monk. Be open to receiving the spirits from the white light that wish to work with you and the most appropriate ones for each healing will come.

Guides can be in many places at once. Jesus is probably the most called upon healer on the planet, yet he still comes for all who call. Call in the guides and Masters who want to help you and you will receive exactly the energy that you need.

Seeing Your Reiki Guides

You are working on an intuitive level with your Reiki guides and may be aware of certain Reiki guides or energies that are working with you. Some people are very sensitive to these spirit energies and can see them clairvoyantly or can feel their presence. Others may be receiving or hearing messages, feeling prompted to move hand positions, or just receiving little "knowings." Don't worry if you are not feeling or sensing your guides. Once you have been attuned through Reiki and you have started your session by calling in your guides and Masters, they are working through you, whether you are consciously aware of it or not.

It is not that the Reiki energy is stronger when channeled through one practitioner or another. It is that some practitioners can feel this energy moving through them more than others. If a person is generally more sensitive to people and crowds, and they take on other people's emotions or are empathic, then they are more likely to "feel" the presence of their guides and to feel the Reiki energy more. Other Reiki practitioners can have the same energy channeling through them and provide the same results for their clients, but may not be aware or feel this energy running through them. Do not question the strength of the Reiki. The strength of the Reiki is from the guides that are working with you and believe me, it is strong whether you feel it or not.

Some people are naturally "visual" and will tend to develop their clairvoyant abilities more quickly. That is they will see auras, colors of pain or healing, and they may even see their guides clairvoyantly standing at the foot of their recipient or working next to them. Others are naturally attuned to sound and may develop their clairaudient abilities more quickly, receiving messages from their guides or "hearing" their guides talk to them.

We all have each of these senses, we just develop them or use them differently. Some people are simply not as sensitive as others, so don't feel inadequate or that your Reiki sessions are not as strong as others if you are not seeing, hearing, or feeling the presence of your guides. They are there.

Reiki Guides Through Attunement

I have found from experience that many of the guides that help me in my Reiki sessions and attunements are also experienced by my students in their own Reiki sessions. I didn't think about it initially but it makes sense that since my students are attuned by me, they will be working with some of the same Reiki spirits that work through me. This may also be a reason that you are drawn to study under a specific Reiki Master. I, of course, in turn have received the connection with many of my Reiki helpers through my Auntie Pauline who attuned me.

Reiki Guide Meditation

This is a meditation to help you meet your Reiki guide.

Prepare – Find a place where you can meditate quietly without being disturbed. Sit comfortably (not lying down where you might actually fall asleep). Light a white candle and place it in front of you.

Protect – Visualize a bright star in the sky and this star's white rays of light beaming down on top of your head. Imagine this white healing light coming down over your shoulders, slowly down over your body, and completely enveloping your entire body with pure white energy in the highest of goodness. Then imagine tree roots of white light going from the soles of your feet down into Mother Earth. You are now protected in this bubble of white light energy where only good energies can come into your aura.

Breathing/Relaxation – Sitting comfortably, place your hands, palms upwards, on your lap. Concentrate on your breathing, taking a deep breath in from your nose, holding for a second, then exhaling long and forcefully through your mouth. With each breath out, envision releasing negative energy and relaxing deeper and deeper.

Connect – Call in the Reiki energy. Tap three times on your Crown Chakra, asking your Reiki guides to connect to you. Tap three times in your left palm and then three times in your right palm with the same intention. Hold your palms out (turned up) and ask the Reiki energy to flow. You may at this point feel buzzing or heat in your palms.

When you are ready for the meditation, you may begin. (You may want a friend to read this aloud to you or familiarize yourself first so that you don't need to read this during the meditation).

Meet Your Reiki Guide Meditation

Imagine that you are staying in a cottage in the woods. You wake up and open the door. It is a beautiful morning. The birds are singing and the sun is shining down on you. You decide to take a walk. You go out of the cottage and follow a footpath through the woods. The sun is warm on your neck but not too hot. It is a beautiful day and you are surrounded by nature. Take a moment to appreciate this scene of wonderful beauty.

As you walk down this path you see a clearing in the woods ahead. As you approach, you see that in the middle of this clearing is a bubbling brook. Along the bank of this brook you see an old oak tree. Sit underneath this tree for a moment and listen to the sound of the rushing water.

Lean down and pick out a special stone. This will be your magical Reiki healing stone. Wash your Reiki stone in the water. Let the fresh clean water wash over your Reiki stone and see it sparkling back at you. Then, as you sit by the brook appreciating the beauty, ask that your Reiki guide come sit beside you.

Feel their presence next to you. You may not see them at first. You may just feel a loving presence. Look down at their feet and notice what they are wearing. As you move up their body, see their clothes and get a sense of who they are. They may have been incarnated (or lived) on earth before. Try to get a sense of when that was. Ask what kind of personality they have and notice what you sense from them (e.g. serious, fun, loving, healing, wise, etc). Ask their hair color. Ask their eye color. Ask if you can be told their name.

Feel the love they are sending you. Thank them for helping you and working with you. Ask if they have a message for you about the Reiki journey you are now embarking upon. Listen for an answer. End by thanking your Reiki guide for being with you and say goodbye for now. Know that your Reiki guide remains close to you and you can come back to this special place and speak with them.

Now it's time to go. Imagine leaving your special place and walking back down the path to the cottage. Enter the cottage and sit down in a chair. Then slowly see yourself back in your seated position in your own room. Imagining a white light that goes down through your spine to the ground, keeping you firmly grounded in this world. When you awake, you will feel refreshed and ready to take on your life challenges, knowing that your Reiki guide is with you.

Now slowly open your eyes.

What did you experience? Did it feel like you were making it up? It often feels like it was just your imagination. That's ok. You will learn from experience that it is not.

I find that it is difficult to visualize my guides straight on. I have an easier time asking to see their profile or asking to see a specific feature such as hair or eye color. Some people cannot visualize anything at all. If you can't, then ask yourself, "Did I sense a loving energy?" "Did I see a color of light?" Your psychic senses are still developing over time and each time you do this meditation, a little more may be revealed to you. You can also ask to see some of your other guides, as you have many waiting to meet you.

CHAPTER 8

CHAKRAS, AURAS, & ENERGY FIELDS

OUR BODIES AS ENERGY BODIES

Science tells us that all physical matter is made up of atoms vibrating at various frequencies. Our body is almost entirely space but appears solid due to the energy vibration of the atoms that we are made of. Not only is our physical body made up of energy, but we also have an energetic aura which is a larger outer body that is invisible to the naked eye. Our bodies and auras live in an energy matrix or grid that runs around the earth and connects us to the earth as well as to one another. Our energy is fed by the energy source, the Chi (or Ki) that runs through us; the life force or God energy.

Chakras

Chakras are widely accepted as fact in many parts of the world. They are of importance in acupuncture and eastern medicine, and can also be seen in various cultures. There are seven main chakras in the body as well as many smaller, less significant ones. The lesser chakras include ones in the palms of the hand that are very important in Reiki and other hands-on healing modalities. Each chakra is an energy center and is associated with different emotions, physical organs, and spiritual relevances. Imagine it as an energy that starts as a pinpoint inside the body and then emanates out as a cone, getting wider as it comes out of both the front and the back of our body. Each chakra vibrates at its own frequency and, therefore, is more tuned into a specific color in the spectrum.

Within each chakra the energy is circulating. When operating at its most efficient, it is clear and bright, and the energy is rotating in a smooth circular motion. It will either rotate clockwise or counterclockwise, whichever is correct for that individual, as well as at the right speed for them. The following are the colors, locations (front and back), and associations for each chakra.

7th Chakra – Crown Chakra

- Color – Purple
- Location – The top of the head, vertical, going up to the sky and through the body.
- Association – Connection to Divine Source

6th Chakra – Third Eye

- Color – Indigo (dark blue)
- Location – Front: in the center of the forehead. Back: at the back of the head.
- Association – Psychic abilities, clairvoyance

5th Chakra – Throat Chakra

- Color – Turquoise blue
- Location – Front: the neck/throat. Behind: at the back of the neck.
- Association – Communication, physical and spiritual

4th Chakra – Heart Chakra

- Color – Emerald Green
- Location – Front: in the center of the chest. Back: in between the shoulder blades.
- Association – Emotions

3rd Chakra – Solar Plexus

- Color – Yellow
- Location – Front: center of diaphragm. Back: mid-back
- Association – God center, how people see us.

2nd Chakra – Sacral Chakra

- Color – Orange
- Location – Front: two inches below the navel. Back: lower back
- Association – Relationships, money

1st Chakra – Base Chakra

- Color – Red
- Location – Vertical, between the legs going down to the ground, as well as up through the body.
- Association – Family, early childhood, how we see ourselves.

8th Chakra – Spiritual Halo

- Color – Gold
- Location – This chakra only develops as you become spiritually connected. It appears as a halo six inches above the crown. Eventually it grows down as a circular umbrella.
- Association – Spiritual connection

Blocked Chakras

If we have attracted negative energy into our auras we may have clouded, slowed, blocked, or even shut down our chakras. When our chakras are working efficiently, they are bright beautiful lights rotating in the correct speed and direction for us.

Auras

Each of us has an energy aura that is a larger outer body that is invisible to the naked eye. This aura is made up of many layers of energy. Although we talk about three main layers of energy and their frequency, there are many more layers extending further out. In addition, there are no defining lines as to where one energy changes to the next. Rather it is a progression of frequencies in grades, each aura running into the next. Consider a rainbow where the colors gradually move from one to the other. There is also no cut-off of energy defining where our energy stops, but rather there is a gradual diminishing of energy. The more powerful and healthy our energy centers are, the larger our aura is. It may be from just a few inches when it is weak, to ten or twelve feet when it is very strong. The main auras that we discuss in Reiki are:

> The aura is made up of many layers of energy. Although we talk about three main layers of energy and their frequency, there are many more layers extending further out.

Emotional Body, Aura

This is the first aura above the physical body. It is located about two inches above the physical body and is where we store emotional energies. Difficult emotional issues may be stored here and, if not resolved, may move closer to the body and develop into physical issues.

Mental Body, Aura

This is the second aura above the physical body. It is located about four inches above the physical body and is where we store mental energies. Difficult issues that we are thinking about may be stored here and, if not resolved, may move closer to the body; first into the emotional body and then to the physical body.

Spiritual Body, Aura

This is the third aura above the physical body. It is located about six inches above the physical body and is where we store spiritual energies. Our life lessons from past lives or our predetermined lessons for this life may be stored here. If not resolved, negative issues may move closer to the body; first into the mental body, then into the emotional body, and then to the physical body.

Progression of Illness

Illnesses may start in our outer auras, either from energy brought over from past life karma or brought into this life by our selection of lessons. In other words, before we come into this life, we have predetermined difficult life lessons and physical illnesses that lie dormant in our outer bodies. Then at some point, this energy is manifested into our lives and becomes part of our mental thoughts or thinking process. That is, we are thinking negative thoughts which affect our emotions and we start to create this negative energy in our life through our emotional state. Eventually this emotional imbalance is drawn further into our energy and becomes a physical illness or issue.

If we are aware of this progression, we can start to work on our issues as we recognize them in our mental thought process and emotions before they ever become a physical issue. We can even heal them in our spiritual outer aura before they ever manifest closer into our other auras.

Of course we may not be aware of bringing negative energy into our lives. Sometimes these energies may even appear quite positive at first. For instance, consider that you have decided that you wish to experience "self love" and have brought over this learning lesson into this life where it is sitting in your outer aura. Then you meet your "soul mate" or this wonderful person that you know you have a spiritual connection with and you are open and willing to become involved. At some point later the relationship turns sour and this person is able to press your buttons and hurt you more than anyone. You are thinking negative thoughts and have brought this energy into your Mental Body. As you remain in this situation and don't learn your lesson, you begin to feel negative emotionally. You have now brought this into your Emotional Body. If this progresses, you may actually develop a physical illness. This physical illness could be related to your Sacral Chakra (relationship energy center) and manifest as a health issue in the reproductive organs. Or it could be related to your Heart Charka or perhaps even another chakra. Eventually you may realize your lesson of self-love that you intended to learn in the first place. Wouldn't it be much easier to release that lesson long before it progressed so far! Reiki can help in releasing these negative energies, even from the very first outer auras.

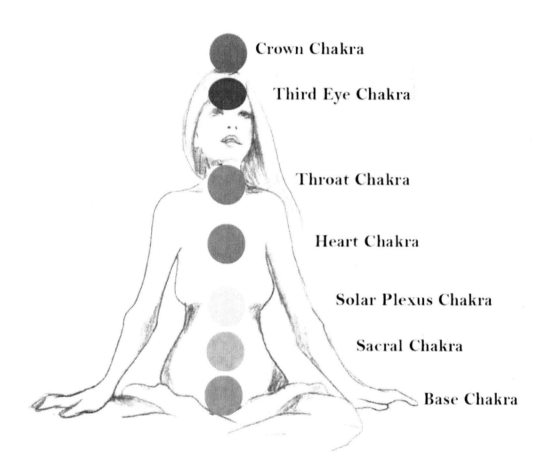

Crown Chakra

Third Eye Chakra

Throat Chakra

Heart Chakra

Solar Plexus Chakra

Sacral Chakra

Base Chakra

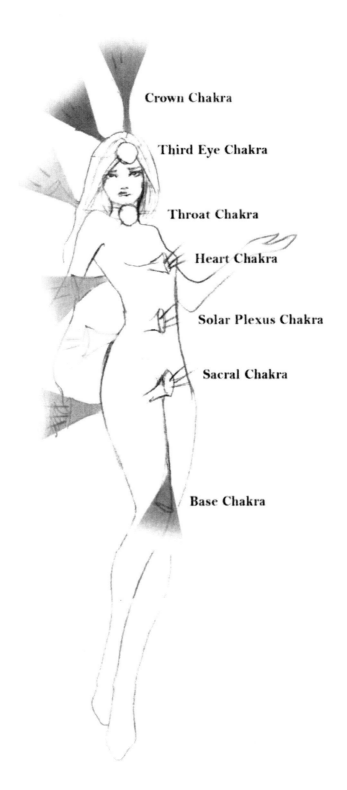

Crown Chakra

Third Eye Chakra

Throat Chakra

Heart Chakra

Solar Plexus Chakra

Sacral Chakra

Base Chakra

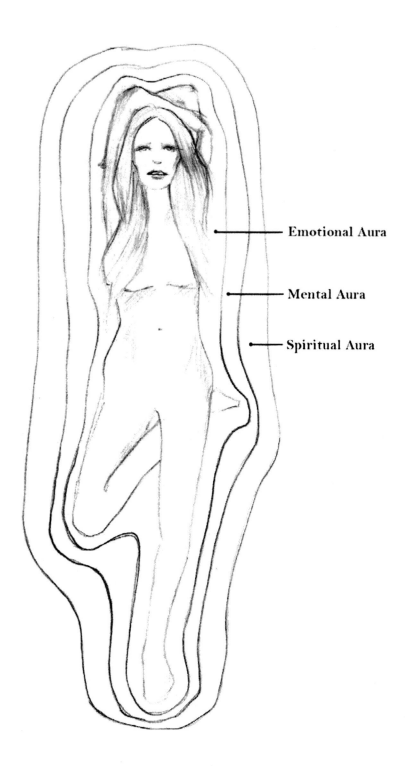

Emotional Aura

Mental Aura

Spiritual Aura

CHAPTER 9
PSYCHIC SENSES

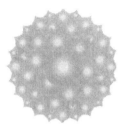

A Reiki attunement will open you up psychically. During an attunement, Reiki flows through you, opening and energizing your chakras. Sacred Reiki symbols are also placed into your chakras. People often report a marked increase in their psychic abilities, especially when giving a Reiki session. Some may start seeing auras or energy colors, or begin to hear messages or receive thoughts. Others report sensing or feeling the area of the body to concentrate on. Some even report seeing their guides and spirits of their recipient.

Types of Psychic Senses

Just like there are the different physical senses (i.e. taste, touch, smell), there are different psychic senses. Usually people connect more with a particular type of psychic sense and it is easier for them to receive messages via that modality. For example, some people are naturally "visual" and will tend to develop their clairvoyant or psychic seeing abilities more quickly. That is they will see auras and energy colors of pain or healing. They may even see their guides or loved ones clairvoyantly. Others are more naturally attuned to sound and may develop their clairaudient abilities more quickly, receiving messages from their guides or "hearing" their guides talk to them.

We all have each of these senses, we just develop them or use them differently. Some people are simply not as sensitive as others, so don't feel inadequate or that you are not as strong as others if you are not seeing, hearing, or feeling the presence of your guides or loved ones. They are there.

The names of the paranormal senses are derived from the French word "clair" meaning "clear" and the translation of the specific sense. For example, the word "voyant" means "seeing" so the term clairvoyant translates as "clear seeing."

Clairvoyance (Seeing)

The clairvoyant sense is the psychic visual sense. Clairvoyance is associated with the Third Eye (6th chakra). Additional chakras related to clairvoyance are the Heart Chakra (4th Chakra) and the Sacral Chakra (2nd chakra). People who are more clairvoyant may see visions of spirits, auras around people, and other paranormal visual experiences.

Clairaudience (Hearing)

The clairaudient sense is hearing psychically. It is associated with the Throat Chakra (5th chakra). Additional chakras related to clairaudience are the Third Eye (6th Chakra) and the Base Chakra (1st chakra). People who are more clairaudient receive messages from spirits. They "hear" or receive thoughts connected with the paranormal.

Clairsentience (Feeling)

The clairsentient sense is feeling psychically. It is associated with the Solar Plexus (3rd chakra). Additional chakras related to clairsentience are the Heart Chakra (4th Chakra) and the Sacral Chakra (2nd chakra). People who are more clairsentient feel things psychically. They often can sense the emotions of others and they receive "gut feelings" or messages.

Clairalience (Smelling)

The clairalient sense is the paranormal sense of smell. It is associated with the Third Eye (6th chakra). People who are more clairalient may smell the perfume of a loved one, grandma's cookies, or the cigar smoke of a passed-over uncle.

Claircognizance (Knowing)

The claircognizant sense is precognition or a "knowing" psychically. It is associated with the solar plexus chakra (3rd chakra). Also related to claircognizance is the Heart Chakra (4th Chakra). People who are more claircognizant often they report to "just know" things. They may have a sense that something is about to happen.

Clairgustance (Tasting)

The clairgustant sense is the paranormal sense of taste. It is associated with the Throat Chakra (5th chakra). Also related to clairgustance is the Third Eye (6th Chakra). People who are more clairgustant may suddenly taste the cooking of a person in spirit or their favorite dessert. They may get a bitter or sweet taste as a psychic sign.

Sensing Energy and Auras

We each have an energy field around us that extends three to six feet. It may be extremely large (e.g. twelve feet) for someone that is highly developed spiritually and maybe very small (e.g. less than two feet) for someone who is suffering, depressed, or in poor health.

To see auras we are using our clairvoyant or "seeing" sense.

If we quiet our mind and get into a meditative state, we can sense or see other people's energy fields. To see auras, we are using our clairvoyant or "seeing" sense. It is best to squint the eyes slightly and look through your peripheral vision. You may actually see a glow or double image around the person and see a color. Or the name of the color may pop into your head if you are more clairaudient.

In a perfectly healthy body and enlightened individual you may see the aura as all white. You may also see pink for love or green for healing. Violet around the head shows connection to the Divine. Most auras have multiple colors and as long as they are vibrant and clear, that is best. Colors like a muddy-red, muddy-orange, grey, black, or a murky color indicate that there is a problem. When the body is healthy, it has an even glow throughout the aura. Breaks in the aura, spots of grey or black, or muddled colors show issues.

You can scan a person's body either visually or by using your hands to scan the energy field a few inches above the physical body. You can actually feel hot spots or changes in energy. However most people, even if they feel this, don't trust it and shrug it off as simply their imagination. I am a great believer in saying the first thing that pops into your head, just having a go at it, or making something up. Often this turns out to be very accurate. When doing the body scan you can tune into your clairsentient sense and feel the changes of the energy with your hands. You may even detect what is causing it. Or as you scan you may feel changes in your own body as guidance as to your client's issue. For example, your elbow starts to ache or your knee itches. It isn't that you have suddenly developed an ache or itch, rather it is an indication being shown to you through your clairsentient sense of where or what to focus on for your client.

CHAPTER 10
RECEIVING PSYCHIC MESSAGES

AReiki attunement enhances your psychic senses and you may immediately start seeing or hearing things psychically. As you practice Reiki, you are working with Spirit and opening your psychic senses. You will become more familiar with your guides and enhance your connection to the other side.

As a side product of Reiki, you may start to receive messages from loved ones. What you are doing is tapping into a higher vibration in the spiritual realm where you are able to sense and talk to people who have passed over. Your relatives or the relatives of your recipient might start to appear to you, either clairvoyantly (meaning you actually see a visual of them), or you may get a thought or feeling that they are there.

This doesn't mean that these spirits are working with you on the healings. It is possible but very unlikely. Spirits of loved ones come through whenever they get the opportunity to do so through someone who can hear them. They are coming through mostly just to tell your recipient that they are ok, that there is in fact an afterlife, and to send their relative love. Occasionally they may give a little message or insight for your recipient, but mostly they are just there as reassurance and to send love.

It is difficult for spirits to come through to people. Don't worry if you feel like you aren't receiving the messages. Mediumship is not always developed right away.

However, as you become more open and can raise your vibrational energy, loved ones will try to come through you. Of course this goes for your own relatives, too. Though often we discount this as just our imagination.

If you want to be a stronger medium but feel it is not happening, be patient. It may develop over time. As you go through the levels of Reiki, the attunements will increase this ability. Practicing with Reiki energy will increase it as well. One thing I have found is to not be afraid. If you have a recipient that will allow you to practice using your mediumship skills, have a go. Say what you think or try just making something up. You'll be amazed at the results.

A Reiki attunement enhances your psychic senses.

CHAPTER 11
ATTUNEMENTS

Reiki attunements are a powerful spiritual initiation. This is the heart of Reiki. The attunement energy is divinely inspired and originates from Divine Source itself. The Reiki attunement is a transfer of energy through the Master to the student with the attunement being given by the Reiki Master's guides in spirit. It aligns the student with the Universal Life Force Energy of Reiki and allows Reiki energy to channel through the body of the student.

What To Expect

Normally students are seated in a chair for the attunement. The student begins with their hands in prayer position over their Heart Chakra. I like to smudge my student with sage smoke (if they have agreed first that this is something they would like). The student is instructed to keep their eyes closed during the entire attunement process. If they are very uncomfortable with this, they can focus straight ahead at a crystal or candle flame. The student is instructed to imagine Reiki energy flowing through them, coming down from their Crown Chakra, running through their body, and expanding out into their aura.

Group or Individual

I personally prefer to perform individual attunements. I take each student into a separate area where I give them their attunement. Some Masters attune their students in groups where the students are lined up in rows or in a small circle. If attunements are given in a group and some are attuned before the others are finished, all must remain in quiet meditation until the whole group is finished.

Distant Attunements

Although most people prefer to receive their attunement in person with a Reiki Master, a student can also be attuned through a distant attunement. I do this occasionally for students who cannot attend a workshop. Although it would seem that this wouldn't work as well, a distant attunement is just as powerful. I arrange a time with my student and have them sit in meditation while I perform the attunement from a distance. It can also be passed through a video. The student may have all the same sensations during and in the days following as if they received an in-person attunement. Of course, if you receive a distant attunement and then get the opportunity later to have one in person, you can always do another attunement at the same level.

Experiences during an attunement

What a student experiences during an attunement is similar to that of a recipient during a Reiki session but stronger. Although some students will feel nothing, the majority of students will feel or experience their attunement.

Physical Sensations – You may feel heat, cold, or tingling sensations. For example, you may feel a muscle twitch or you may sweat.

Dizziness – Occasionally students feel slightly dizzy. If this happens, just relax and your Reiki Master may instruct you to visualize tree roots of white light going down into Mother Earth to ground you.

Emotionally Overwhelmed – the Reiki energy may bring up and resolve issues within you as it clears your chakras. You may even see a glimpse of a past life or your soul purpose. It may also be a very happy emotion that makes you want to cry. Emotions are good. Allow yourself to release.

Laughing or Crying – You may experience uncontrollable giggling, laughter, or may even want to cry. Just accept and allow yourself to feel what ever you are experiencing.

Seeing Colors – Some sense bright lights or balls of light. This is simply the Reiki energy coming into you and your clairvoyant sense powering up. You may even see visions or receive messages.

Seeing Spirits – Some may see their guides or Reiki Masters in spirit. Students may even see Dr. Usui during an attunement.

After an Attunement

Immediately following any Reiki attunement there is a period where the cleansing can be intense. This often coincides with the 21 days of self-healing. Your guides continue to clear your chakras and align your energy during this period. If you had blockages (physical or spiritual), your Reiki guides will remove these blockages first. As your chakras are cleansed and aligned, anything that you didn't deal with may surface. This is a good thing as you are finally resolving and releasing negative energies that may have been causing you issues for years.

Cleansing takes place on all levels – physical, mental, emotional, and spiritual. The more the Reiki energy is allowed to flow, the more beneficial this will be. During this time, go easy on yourself and allow the process. Drink lots of water as this will help you to release toxins and flush out any negative energy that has surfaced. Your self-healing sessions will help you to release and cleanse more quickly. Take time to meditate daily. Allow yourself lots of sleep and rest. Taking walks in nature is very healing and may help you through this process.

Most students report some moments of emotion during this time. They usually report feeling wonderful, more energetic, healthy, and alive.

> During an attunement you may feel heat, cold, or tingling sensations.

Preparation Before an Attunement

Some preparation the week before will help you to get the strongest connection out of your attunement. However, even if you don't do any preparation, you will still receive the energies, become a Reiki channel, and receive your Reiki Level One certificate. Your Reiki powers will also continue to enhance long after the class. These suggestions are not something to stress over, but if you have the time they may help strengthen your initial experience and minimize any negative feelings afterwards.

I usually send my students an email with notes to prepare for the class. Here are some preparation guidelines to help you get the most out of your attunement. Basically they are meant to clear your body and soul, and help you to get to your peak psychic acceptance.

Preparation for an Attunement

1. Limit or cut out animal protein for the 3 days prior. Fish is fine. This is to clear any negative energies from food.

2. If you have ever fasted and enjoy this process, fasting on juice or water beforehand is good. (1-2 days or just a few hours). If you are not used to this then just try to eat healthy.

3. Limit or stop any caffeinated drinks for 3 days.

4. Limit or no alcohol for 3 days.

5. Limit or no sugar or junk food for 3 days.

6. Limit or stop smoking cigarettes for 3 days.

7. Quiet negative outside distractions, news, horror movies, etc. for 3 days.

8. Try to spend some time appreciating nature each day.

9. Start as soon as possible and meditate daily, an hour if possible. If you are not able to meditate, just sit quietly and contemplate. Ask to release anger, fear, worry, and other negative feelings. Then spend some time contemplating or meditating on why you want to receive a Reiki attunement and what you wish to receive from your Reiki attunement. (e.g. to increase your psychic ability or to be able to heal yourself and others, mentally and physically, etc.)

10. If you use other rituals or methods to get your psychic powers stimulated, go ahead and start to prepare yourself. (e.g. crystals)

Again, many people do nothing beforehand, so don't stress about this, but a quiet contemplating period before would be good and at least avoid a heavy party weekend!

CHAPTER 12

PROTECTION AND GROUNDING

In opening up to the other side, we want to make sure we are only connecting with the highest beings that can guide and help us in a positive way.

It is important to protect yourself psychically before commencing any type of spiritual work. This is because you are connecting to the other side and you want to make sure you are only connecting with spirits from the white light and of the highest of intentions. This is not intended to alarm you, but it is worth knowing and taking the proper precautions. In the physical world we have people that are predominantly good and have the highest of intentions, as well as those that are not as spiritually evolved and have a lower vibrational energy. There are also all shades in between. We may have the impression that on the other side, all spirits are good. However, the other side it is very similar to the physical plane with all variations of positive and negative. There are spirits that are evolved and those that are still going through heavy lessons. In opening up to the other side, we want to make sure we are only connecting with the highest beings that can guide and help us in a positive way.

Some people believe that protection is not necessary since our guides and angels are already looking over us and so we are always divinely protected. My experience is that if I forget to protect myself, I may feel drained, tired, or even get a headache, so I believe it is always best to protect oneself. It only takes a few minutes.

There are many methods of protection. Most involve visualization and asking God, your angels, or Divine beings to protect you. You may envision a ball of protective white light around you, a barrier of emotional protection around you, or stepping into a protective psychic suit.

Here is a simple bubble of white light protection that I personally use:

Bubble of White Light Protection

Visualize a bright star in the sky coming toward you and then hovering over your head. Imagine its white rays of light beaming down on top of your head with a warm loving energy. Imagine this white healing light coming down over your shoulders, down over your body, and as it touches each part you, feel relaxed, loved, and protected. Allow this energy to completely envelop your entire body with pure white light energy in the highest of goodness. You are now protected in this bubble of white light energy where only good energies can come into your aura.

Grounding

Make sure you are grounded before giving a Reiki session. If you do not ground yourself you may feel "spacey," forgetful, or disoriented after the session. During your protection, simply visualize tree roots of white light going down from the soles of your feet into Mother Earth, connecting you and grounding you.

CHAPTER 13

PREPARING YOUR SPACE

You should have already prepared your space before your recipient arrives, making sure it is protected and energized. If I have prepared my space much earlier, I will do a quick preparation or review just before I start the session.

Call In Your Reiki Energy

I do my bubble of white light protection and then call in my Reiki energy.

Sage

I use sage for smudging in the corners of the room. I light a sage wand and then with the smoke, I make counterclockwise circles in each corner. I then go around my Reiki bed (or chair) and repeat this with the sage smoke over each corner of the bed. Make sure you have a window or door slightly cracked for the smoke to leave. Smudging with sage is a Native American tradition. They believe the smoke from the sage collects any negative spirits, earthbound spirits, or negative energies, so you want this smoke to leave your room along with the negativity.

Incense

It is great to burn incense such as sandalwood that attracts positive spirits. Sweet grass is also wonderful for this.

Herbs

I like to place fresh herbs that I have picked, such as rosemary, lavender, and lemon verbena.

Candles

Invoke white light energy with candles. Light a purple candle and a white candle. Ask the purple flame to consume any negative energies and transmute them to positive energy, and the white candle to represent the light from the Divine Source. I prefer to have the room lights dimmed as well.

You should have already prepared your space before your recipient arrives, making sure it is protected and energized.

Crystals

I like to place a large crystal in the healing room somewhere. I energize the crystal with Reiki energy and ask my crystal to keep sending Reiki to the room and to my recipient.

Music

If you are using music, set it to a low volume and make sure it is a relaxing selection. Set it to repeat so that you will not have to change it during a session.

Temperature

Make sure the temperature of your room is comfortable for your recipient.

Water

Make sure you have water available for your recipient after the session. You should encourage them to drink lots of fresh water.

CHAPTER 14

CALLING IN REIKI ENERGY

You are now attuned to Reiki energy and have Reiki guides and Masters in spirit waiting to work with you. This energy will always be available to you for the rest of your life.

You do not need to force or "send" Reiki, simply allow it to flow through you. Imagine you are a hollow cylinder or channel and that Spirit is simply using your physical body. You do not need to concentrate or meditate to give Reiki. Some practitioners feel the energy flowing through them more than others. This is simply the sender's own personal sensitivity to feeling the energy and it does not mean that the recipient receives any greater or lesser energy.

To start a session:

Protect Yourself

First protect yourself psychically by imagining a ball of white light coming over you. Another variation some people like is to imagine stepping into a golden suit of protection and zipping it up. Find what works best for you. You are invoking protection from Divine Source. DO NOT SKIP THIS. Be sure to ground yourself during this by visualizing tree roots of white light going down into Mother Earth.

Find Your Still Place

Make sure you are in a quiet, relaxed, and receptive state. Give yourself plenty of time. You should have meditated earlier, if not right before. Make sure you are ready mentally.

Call In Your Reiki Guides

Connect with your Reiki guides. Tap three times on your crown with the intention that you are making a connection to the spirit world and asking your Reiki energy to flow. Tap three times on the palm of your left hand and then tap three times on the right. Put your hands out and turn your hands, palms facing up. Ask the Reiki energy to flow. You may actually feel a signal that your Reiki energy is turning on. For me, I feel a definite energy surge with a tingly feeling coming from the center of my palms. As you go though higher levels of Reiki you will learn symbols to enhance this power up. But even at level I, you may feel the Reiki energy turning on. If you don't feel anything, don't worry; it is still working. Just continue with your session.

You are now ready to begin.............

Switching Off Your Reiki

After a session, always remember to disconnect your energy from your recipient. You can do this just by telling your guides the session is now finished. I sometimes do a chopping motion with my hand in front of me, as if cutting any connection. Then reaffirm your own bubble of white light. Thank your Reiki guides and Masters for working with you.

CHAPTER 15

SELF-HEALING

One of the great advantages of the Reiki healing system is that the sender receives the benefits of the Reiki energy as they allow the energy to flow through them. They do not feel tired or drained after "giving" a Reiki session. In fact, they will usually feel energized.

21 SELF-HEALING SESSIONS

Before you start working on others (except during this class) you need to do 21 self-healing sessions. This is so the spirits can work on you as a channel, opening all your chakras and clearing your energy. We need to be a clear and open channel in order to allow the Reiki energy to flow through us and be delivered to our recipient. The sessions will concentrate on each of the seven main chakras for three sessions each, starting at the Base Chakra. As this is done, you may feel any unresolved issues related to those chakras being brought to the surface for review and release. For example, during sessions four, five, and six, while spirit is working on your Sacral Chakra (2nd chakra), you may find yourself thinking about unresolved relationship issues. When your Heart Chakra is being worked on, you may find yourself being more emotional. After you have done your initial twenty one self-healing sessions don't forget to give yourself regular tune-ups, and not just when you feel you really need it.

> After you have done your initial twenty one self-healing sessions don't forget to give yourself regular tune-ups...

Some have asked what happens if you do a session on a friend before your twenty one self-healing sessions are complete. It cannot harm the recipient as there is no such thing as harmful Reiki. You may simply not yet be as clear a channel as you would like, and the Reiki may be slower or weaker.

CONDUCTING A SELF-HEALING SESSION

Be Relaxed

Please don't do any type of meditation or spiritual connection when you still feel rushed from something else you were doing. Try to give yourself plenty of time beforehand so that you can calm yourself, relax, and feel unrushed. Also, always wash your hands before you begin, as this is a psychic message that you are cleansing your body and allowing for the clear path of Reiki.

Prepare Your Space

You should have already prepared your area. Just because this session is just for yourself doesn't mean you can skip this step. I make sure my space is protected and energized. I use sage for smudging in the corners. If I already completely prepared my space some time earlier, I will just do a quick preparation before I start the session. Invoke white light energy with candles and Reiki energy. Light a purple candle and a white candle. Ask the purple flame to consume any negative energies and transmute them to positive energy and the white candle to represent the light from Divine Source. If you are playing music, choose a relaxing selection. Set it to a low volume and to repeat so that you will not have to change it.

Meditation

When Dr. Usui says for today to "work hard" he is referring to spiritual work, including daily meditation. I recommend finding time each day to meditate and connect with your Spirit Guides and Ascended Reiki Masters (Reiki Masters in spirit). Meditation is a very personal practice and if you are not experienced with it, try some different examples and see what works best for you. I usually meditate for at least thirty minutes at the beginning of the day, as there is not always time to do this right before giving a Reiki session. So, I will do a more complete meditation earlier in the day and then just run through a quick meditation right before the session begins. Develop your own meditation practice to connect yourself to your guides and become spiritually in tune. Make sure you include grounding in your meditation.

Get Comfortable

Make yourself comfortable. You can either do the hand positions while lying down or you can do them from a seated position. You may want to do a self-healing in bed before you go to sleep. If you are so comfortable that you fall asleep during the session that is ok. Your guides will continue to work on you. Perhaps you would like to do a self-healing in a seated position before you start your day. Follow your intuition and guidance.

Protection

I always use protection. This consists of at least calling in the white light and seeing myself standing completely protected in a bubble or cloak of white light, stating that I am protected by Divine light. Do not skip this. You need to protect yourself psychically even if it is done quickly because you are opening up your senses to receive spiritual input from outside of yourself. This is to make sure that only good energy comes into your aura.

Call In Your Reiki Guides and Masters

Starting with your hands in prayer position over your Heart Chakra, ask that your Ascended Reiki Masters, spirit guides, angels and all energies from the white light who wish to help heal you, come in now. At this point you can call in specific energies as well, if you wish.

State Your Intention

Intention is extremely important. In fact, to me it is the number one secret to making your Reiki strong. At this point, state your intention to your spirit guides of what you would like to accomplish. Usually I advise saying this silently in your head to your guides. You may say whatever feels right at the time. You can also make up your own chant or mantra for stating your intention for the session. Here is an example:

"I call in my Reiki Masters and guides as well as any other healing entities from the white light that wish to help me in this Reiki session. May my connection to the Reiki energy be pure and strong. I ask that you use my body as a channel to send Reiki to myself and that I receive this Reiki in my highest of goodness. I ask for healing in the area of [state the specific area or ailment] as well as all the areas where I may need it. I ask that I receive this Reiki energy immediately and in perfect ways."

This is just an example. You can use what feels right to you, but always state that you wish to send Reiki and use the word Reiki throughout your session.

Start the Reiki Flow

Imagine the Reiki energy flowing through the top of your head or Crown Chakra, through your body, and through your palms. You may also tap three times on your crown, then three times in each palm or massage counterclockwise on your palm with your middle finger with the intention of calling in the Reiki energy.

> Intention is extremely important. In fact, to me it is the number one secret to making your Reiki strong.

I then turn my hands, face-up, toward the ceiling and wait a few seconds until I feel the energy flowing through me and to my palms. For me there is a distinct buzzing in my palms and fingertips that tells me the Reiki energy is flowing. It just takes a few seconds to flow once I have asked. Others may feel heat or see white light in their palms. If you don't feel or sense anything, don't worry. It is still working. Just trust that it is there.

Hold your hands over your ears but not touching. You may feel a buzzing in your hands or ears (especially your right ear) or you may feel heat. Hold this for a couple of minutes and then start the self-healing hand positions.

Hand Positions

The hand positions are not given as a strict rule to follow, but rather as a guideline for directing the energy. (See page 64 for photographs of the self-healing hand positions.) Most importantly, the hand positions should be comfortable. If a position is difficult to reach, such as on the back or touching the soles of your feet, one should adapt the position so that it is comfortable. This allows the energy to flow easily.

Hold each hand position for 3-5 minutes. As you hold each position, do not try to force the energy to flow, but rather visualize yourself allowing your body to be used as a channel. Imagine the energy flowing through you. Do not try to direct it. You may feel heat or tingling. Do not feel that you have to do each hand position for precisely 3-5 minutes and then the exact next position as specified. Try to be guided by your intuition and move when you are guided to move. The hand positions do not have to be perfect and you may be directed "off book." Reiki energy is intelligent so the energy will flow to where it is needed, regardless of your hand position. This is why you may feel like your feet are being worked on when, in fact, you are holding your hand over your Heart Chakra.

> The hand positions are not given as a strict rule to follow, but rather as a guideline for directing the energy for overall balance of healing.

If you have a particular affliction you may be guided to focus on that specific area. For example, if you have a headache or are prone to over-thinking, then you may feel the desire to hold the hand positions on the head for longer. Other areas you may feel do not need as much attention. If you are not feeling guided or are unsure, go ahead and do each hand position for 3-5 minutes in the traditional order. After you have given several Reiki sessions you will get more confident in "feeling" the energy and trusting your guidance.

Some hand positions may be difficult for you. If this is the case, it is more important to be comfortable and relaxed than to do the exact position. For instance, if you cannot comfortably place your hands on your lower back just place them at your side and imagine that your hands are on your lower back. Directing the energy with your thoughts is just as effective as placing your hands there. If your session is lying down, for the hand positions over the knees you may be more comfortable if you draw your knees up toward your chest or you may wish to sit up. Again, make sure the position is comfortable or, if not, just imagine you are doing the position and direct the Reiki with your mind.

When you do the hand position holding the soles of your feet, you are completing an energy circuit. Visualize tree roots of white light going from the soles of your feet into Mother Earth to ground you.

> If you don't feel or sense anything, don't worry. It is still working. Just trust that it is there.

Sealing in the Reiki Energy

When you feel you have received enough Reiki and it is time to close, ask that the Reiki energy continue to flow to you after the session for as long as is needed in the highest of goodness. State that the Reiki session is complete.

Thank Your Guides

Ask again for the white light to cover and protect you. Place your hands back in prayer position in front of your Heart Chakra. Thank your Reiki guides and Ascended Masters, spirit guides, and all of the other healers that helped you.

Relax and Drink

Allow yourself to rest and relax for a few moments. Remember to drink lots of water.

Wash Your Hands

Wash your hands before and after your session. This has a spiritual/psychic connotation that you are washing away any negative energies.

Continued Healing

After a session you may find the releasing continues. This may feel uncomfortable as you are asked to deal with issues and emotions that you thought were resolved long ago. This is especially true for your first twenty one self-healing sessions after an attunement. Don't worry if you find yourself feeling a little sad or thinking negative thoughts about an old situation. Realize that this is just part of the process of releasing. If you are feeling particularly dizzy or spacey, make sure you are doing a grounding meditation at beginning of a session or anytime you are feeling spacey.

REIKI SELF-HEALING SESSION CHECKLIST

- Be relaxed
- Prepare Your Space
- Meditate
- Get Comfortable
- Protect
- **Call In** Your Reiki Guides and Masters
- **State Y**our Intention
- **Start th**e Reiki Flow
- **Hand P**ositions
- **Seal in** the Reiki Energy
- **Thank** Your Guides
- **Wash Y**our Hands

SELF-HEALING HAND POSITIONS

You may do these lying down, sitting in a chair, or even standing.

1. *Back of the head* – Place both of your hands on the back of your head in a slight V-shape. The base of your hands be touching the base of your skull and your fingertips should point in and up toward your crown. Imagine yourself as a channel allowing the Reiki energy to flow from your hands to your head. This is soothing and relaxing.

2. *Hands over your crown* – Place your hands over the top of your head with one hand on each side and your fingertips meeting at the top of your head (Crown Chakra). The Reiki energy is working on your mind, head, and crown.

3. *Hands over your eyes* – Cup your hands over your eyes with your fingertips at the top of your forehead. The Reiki energy is working on your eyes and your Third Eye, helping you to see more clearly physically and spiritually.

4. *Hands across the back of your head and neck* – Place your hands side by side on the back of your head. One hand should be at the base of your skull (top of your neck) and the other above (covering the back of your Third Eye). The Reiki energy is working on your mind, head, and Third Eye.

5. *Hands cupped over your throat* – Cup your hands in a V-shape around your throat. You are working on your Throat Chakra, which will enable you to speak more confidently and clearly.

6. *Hands on your shoulders* – Place your hands, one on each shoulder. You may cross your arms if this is more comfortable. (Either way is fine.) This is soothing and releases the stress carried in the shoulders.

7. *Hands over your heart* – Place your hands with your fingertips touching over your Heart Chakra (a little above the center of your chest). The Reiki energy is working on your Heart Chakra.

8. *Hands over your Solar Plexus* – Place your hands with your fingertips touching over your Solar Plexus Chakra just below the center of your chest. The Reiki energy is working on your Solar Plexus Chakra.

9. *Hands over your navel* – Move your hands slightly lower so that your fingertips touch over your navel. You are directing Reiki to your internal organs.

10. *Hands over your Sacral Chakra* – Place your hands on either side of your groin area. The base of your hands should be on or near the hip bones and your fingertips should be over the pubic bone. You are directing Reiki to your Sacral Chakra.

11. *Hands over your lower back* – Slide your hands behind you to rest at your lower back (just above your hips). Your fingers should be pointing downward and touching the upper buttocks. (For the lying down position, if it is easier, you may lean forward resting your weight on your elbows as you place your hands underneath your lower back.) You are directing Reiki to the back of your Sacral Chakra.

12. *Hands over your Base Chakra* – Slide your hands underneath each buttock cupping the fold where it meets the top of your leg. If you are lying down it may be easier to draw your knees toward your chest. You are directing Reiki to your Base Chakra.

13. *Hands over your knees* – Place one hand over each of your knees. If you are lying down it may be easier to either draw your knees up toward your chest or to lean forward, covering your knees from a seated position. If you prefer you may just envision that you are touching your knees without actually doing so.

14. *Cup the soles of your feet* – As you cup the soles of your feet visualize tree roots of white light going from your feet into Mother Earth to ground you. This completes the circuit of energy and is very balancing.

SELF-HEALING POSITIONS

1. Back of the head

2. Hands over your crown

3. Hands over your eyes

4. Back of your head and neck

5. Throat Chakra

6. Shoulders

7. Heart Chakra

8. Solar Plexus Chakra

9. Navel

10. Sacral Chakra

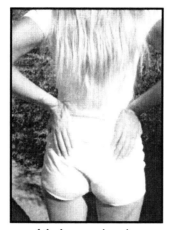
11. Lower back

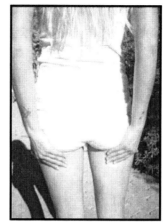
12. Base Chakra

13. Knees

14. Soles of your feet

CHAPTER 16

HEALING OTHERS

I know some of you are very much "by the book" and like to have everything spelled out. I encourage you to start to trust your intuition and make variations as you are guided to by your Reiki guides and Masters. Remember, they are really the ones doing the healing. However, to build your initial confidence, I am giving you a roadmap or plan of action for a Reiki session. This session should take 30-45 minutes.

Be Relaxed

You should not do any type of meditation or spiritual connection when you are still rushed from something else you were doing. Try to give yourself plenty of time beforehand so that you can calm yourself, relax, and feel unrushed. Also, you should always wash your hands before you start. This is not only for proper hygiene, but it is a psychic message that you are cleansing your body and allowing for the clear path of Reiki.

Prepare Your Space

You should have already prepared a massage table, bed, or chair for your session. Make sure that this is not only comfortable for the recipient but also for yourself. You do not want to be bending over in an uncomfortable position throughout the session. I then make sure my space is protected and energized. I use sage for smudging in the corners. If I have already completely prepared my space some time earlier, I will just do a quick preparation before I start the session. Invoke white light energy with candles and Reiki energy. Light a purple candle and a white candle, ask the purple flame to consume any negative energies and transmute them to positive energy and the white candle to represent the light from the Divine Source. If you are playing music, choose a relaxing selection. Set it to a low volume and to repeat so that you will not have to change it.

Meditation

When Dr. Usui says for today to "work hard" he is referring to spiritual work, including daily meditation. I recommend finding time each day to meditate and connect with your Spirit Guides and Ascended Reiki Masters (Reiki Masters in spirit). Meditation is a very personal practice and if you are not experienced with it, try some different examples and see what works best for you. I usually meditate for at least thirty minutes at the beginning of the day, as there is not always time to do this right before giving a Reiki session. So, I will do a more complete meditation earlier in the day and then just run through a quick meditation right before the session begins. Develop your own meditation practice to connect with your guides and become spiritually in tune. Make sure you include grounding in your meditation.

Protection

Always protect yourself. You can do this by calling in the white light and seeing yourself standing in a bubble of white light. State that you are protected by Divine light. Do not skip this. You need to protect yourself psychically, even if it is done quickly. It is not that you are protecting yourself from your recipient specifically (although that too), but you are protecting yourself psychically because you are opening up your senses to receive spiritual input from outside of yourself. You need to make sure that only good energy comes into your aura.

Situate Your Recipient

Briefly explain to your recipient what you are going to be doing. Let them know that you will be placing your hands lightly on them or just above them, discussing what they may feel. Make sure they are not rushed and have time allocated for the full session. Ask your recipient to lay down face-up on your bed (unless you are doing a seated session or have arranged for another position).

It is optional to pass sage smoke around your recipient, the bed, and the area where you are working. Make sure you have their approval beforehand and they know what to expect.

Call In Your Reiki Masters and Guides

Start with your hands in prayer position over your Heart Chakra. Ask that your Ascended Reiki Masters, spirit guides, angels and all energies from the white light who wish to help you heal, come in now. At this point you can call in specific energies as well, if you wish.

State Your Intention

Intention is extremely important. In fact, to me, it is the number one secret to making your Reiki strong. At this point, state your intention to your spirit guides as to what you would like to accomplish. Usually I advise saying this silently in your head to your guides. You may say what ever feels right at the time. You can also make up your own chant or mantra for stating your intention for the session. Here is an example:

> Always protect yourself. You can do this by calling in the white light and seeing yourself standing in a bubble of white light. State that you are protected by Divine light.

> "I call in my Reiki Masters and guides as well as any other healing entities from the white light that wish to help me in this Reiki session. May my connection to the Reiki energy be pure and strong. I ask that you use my body as a channel to send Reiki to my recipient [name] and that they receive this Reiki in their highest of goodness. I ask for healing in the area of [name the specific area or ailment] as well as all the areas that they need it. I ask that they receive this Reiki energy immediately and in perfect ways."

This is just an example. You can use whatever feels right to you, but always state that you wish to send Reiki and use the word Reiki throughout your session.

Start the Reiki Flow

Imagine the Reiki energy flowing through the top of your head or Crown Chakra, through your body, and through your palms. You may also tap three times on your crown, then three times in each palm or massage counterclockwise on your palm with your middle finger with the intention of calling in the Reiki energy.

I then turn my hands, face-up, toward the ceiling and wait a few seconds until I feel the energy flowing through me and to my palms. For me there is a distinct buzzing in my palms and fingertips that tells me the Reiki energy is flowing. It just takes a few seconds to flow once I have asked. Others may feel heat or see white light in their palms. If you don't feel or sense anything, don't worry. It is still working. Just trust that it is there.

Make the Connection With Your Recipient

With your recipient lying face-up on your bed, start with your hands a little above their head by about an inch or two. Your palms should be facing their head but not touching. What you are doing is making a connection with your recipient. Imagine the Reiki energy flowing through the top of your head (Crown Chakra), through your body, and then through your palms to your recipient. Hold this position for a couple of minutes. You may be able to feel or visualize the energy connection. If you can't sense anything, don't worry. You are still connected and you may begin doing the hand positions.

Hand Positions - Recipient Facing Up

Start at your recipient's head, holding each hand position for 3-5 minutes. As you hold each position, do not try to force the energy flow. Visualize yourself allowing your body to be a channel. Imagine the energy flowing through you but do not try to direct it. You may feel heat or tingling. Try to be guided by your intuition and move when you are guided to move. Do not feel like you have to do each hand position for exactly 3-5 minutes and then have to do the next position in the book. The hand positions do not have to be perfect and you may be guided to go "off book." Reiki energy is intelligent so it will flow to where the energy is needed regardless of your hand position. This is why a person may feel that his feet are being worked on when, in fact, the healer is at the Heart Chakra. If however, you are not feeling guided and are unsure, go ahead and do each hand position for 3-5 minutes in the traditional order. After you have given several Reiki sessions you will get more confident in "feeling" the energy and trusting your guidance.

Cleanse and Balance Each Chakra

Once you have finished each hand position with your recipient facing up, you are going to go back over your recipient, cleansing the chakras. Place your hands above each chakra, one at a time. You can start at either the Base Chakra or the Crown Chakra, whichever you prefer. I personally start at the crown. As you place your hands over, and about and inch or two above the chakra, ask for the Reiki to flow through your palms. Visualize the chakra opening up in a beautiful rotating funnel of light, emanating the correct color for that chakra.

You can then use your pendulum (See Chapter 19 for how to use a pendulum) over the chakra to make sure it is open and spinning. If your pendulum is not rotating or rotating very slowly, send Reiki to that chakra for a few more minutes. Try again until the pendulum shows that the chakra is open.

Sweep and Heal the Aura

You are now going to sweep (clear) any negative energy from your recipient's aura. Starting at the head, about two inches away, make sweeping motions with your hands as if you are sweeping away dust and debris. Keep sweeping the psychic dust all the way down to the bottom of their body. When you have collected it at the bottom of the feet, psychically in your imagination, but with hand movements, collect all the psychic dust and pour it into an imaginary bucket. Repeat this again doing a second sweep about four inches above the body. Then do a third sweep about six inches above the body. When all three sweeps have been completed, tip your psychic bucket into the floor and ask that the negative dust go down into Mother Earth to be transmuted into positive energy and come out at the other side of the world where it may give positive energy to the earth. Do not worry about the exact placement of your hands. The intention of removing the psychic dust from the aura and visualizing it is what is most important.

Hand Positions - Recipient Facing Down

Gently ask your recipient to slowly turn over. Assist them in turning if needed. Starting once again at the head, you may follow the hand positions for the back of the body, holding each hand position for 3-5 minutes. As with the front, follow your intuition as to when you should move to the next position or if a slightly altered position is more beneficial. As you do this, keep feeling relaxed and allow the Reiki energy to channel through you. You may get little "knowings," sense things, or actually feel or hear messages from your recipient's passed-over loved ones, as well as your guides. Just allow yourself to feel and sense whatever is given to you. We will work more on the intuitive side of healing at Reiki Level II.

When you get to the last position at the soles of the feet (I like to do this position actually holding and cupping the soles of the feet), imagine grounding your recipient; that the Reiki energy is flowing into the soles of their feet and then out to Mother Earth to connect and ground them. This helps your recipient to not feel so "spacey" when the session is finished.

Cleanse and Balance Each Chakra From the Back

Each chakra is not only at the front of the body but continues through the body to the backside. For instance, the Third Eye Chakra opens at the back of the head as well as in the middle of the forehead. The Throat Chakra comes out at the back of the neck as well as the throat. While your recipient is still lying on their back, place your hands just above each chakra at the backside, one chakra at a time. Again, use the pendulum to check that each chakra is open. Send more Reiki to any chakra that is not open and rotating.

Sweep and Heal the Aura From the Back

You are now going sweep and clear any negative energy from the recipient's aura on the backside of their body. Repeat the three sweeps as detailed in the section above for the recipient's front side.

Sealing In the Reiki Energy

You are now going to seal the Reiki into your recipient's aura. You may stand at the head of your recipient with your hands just above their crown and your palms facing their head, or you may stand at your recipient's feet with your palms facing their feet. Do what feels right to you. Ask to send Reiki to fill your recipient's aura. Imagine the Reiki energy filling up their aura and surrounding them in a bubble of white light. As you do this, silently ask that the Reiki energy continue to flow to your recipient after the session for as long as is needed. State that the Reiki session is completed in the highest of goodness for [recipient name].

Separate Your Energy and Thank Your Guides

Take a step back from your recipient. Imagine your energy is a separate bubble of white light that protects you and is completely separate and disconnected from your recipient. You may move your hands in a cutting motion to cut away any ties and make sure your energy is completely disconnected from theirs. Ask again for the white light to cover you and protect you. Place your hands back in prayer position in front of your Heart Chakra and thank your Reiki guides and Masters, spirit guides, and all other healers that helped you.

Gently Bring Your Recipient Around

Gently and softly tell your recipient that the session is now complete. Allow them to be still and relax for a few moments. When they are "back to earth" you may discuss what they felt and any knowings or feelings that you had during the session. Instruct your recipient to move slowly at first and to drink lots of water.

Wash Your Hands

It is not only hygienic to wash your hands before and after a session so that you don't spread any colds, etc., but it also has a spiritual or psychic connotation that you are washing any negative energies away.

REIKI CLIENT SESSION CHECKLIST

- Be Relaxed

- Prepare Your Space

- Meditate

- Protect

- Situate Your Recipient

- Call In Your Reiki Guides and Masters

- State Your Intention

- Start the Reiki Flow

- Make the Connection With Your Recipient

- Hand Positions Recipient – Facing Up

- Cleanse and Balance Each Chakra

- Sweep and Heal the Aura

- Hand Positions Recipient – Facing Down

- Cleanse and Balance Each Chakra From the Back

- Sweep and Heal the Aura From the Back

- Seal In the Reiki Energy

- Separate Your Energy and Thank Your Guides

- Gently Bring Your Recipient Around

- Wash Your Hands

Variations in a Session

You may find that you are guided to do all the hand positions or you may be guided to skip certain positions and concentrate almost entirely on one or two areas. You may also be guided to do a hand position not in the book. Trust your own inner feelings. These feelings are your guides connecting with you.

You may feel guided to only do the pendulum at the end or perhaps to just check certain chakras. Alternatively, you may be guided to use your pendulum to check your work after each hand position. Do what feels right to you.

Some Reiki healers will only do the aura clearing at the end of the session when the client is backside up, skipping the first one where the client is face-up. The thought here is that the aura clearing encompasses the whole body and not just one side. I recommend that you follow what feels best for you and if you are not sure at first, follow the instructions above and do each side individually.

Be open to following spiritual direction and create your own rapport with your guides.

THE HAND POSITIONS INTEGRATED IN A SESSION

Hand Positions – Face Up

1. *Protect yourself and call in your Reiki*

2. *Connect with your recipient* – Standing behind your recipient, hold your hands a few inches from their head and direct the Reiki energy to them.

3. *Hands cradling the head* – Gently move your recipient's head to one side and place one hand underneath their head. Then roll their head to the other side and slip the other hand underneath. Cradle their head as you channel Reiki energy. Think about allowing the energy to flow through you, relaxing your recipient's mind. When you are done, gently slip your hands out.

4. *Hands over the ears* – Place your hands over their ears. (It is a personal preference whether or not to allow your hands to touch their ears.) You are working on their hearing, physically and emotionally.

5. *Thumbs over the Third Eye* – Place your thumbs together over their Third Eye with your hands over the temples. You are working on opening their Third Eye as well relaxing their mind.

6. *Hands over the eyes* – Place your hands a couple of inches above your recipient's eyes, covering them but not touching. You are working on their eyesight as well as enabling them to see situations more clearly.

7. *Hands cupped over the throat* – Cup your hands in a V-shape around your recipient's throat but not touching it. You are working on their Throat Chakra, which will enable them to speak up more confidently and clearly.

8. *Hands over the heart* – Still in the V-shape, place your hands above your recipient's Heart Chakra. If it is not comfortable to continue standing behind your recipient as you do this hand position, you may stand at their side.

9. *Hands on the shoulders* – Place your hands, one on each shoulder. You may touch your recipient if you prefer. This is soothing and releases the stress carried in the shoulders.

10. *Balancing the head and the heart* – Gently move your recipient's head to one side and place one hand underneath. As you cradle their head with the one hand, place the other hand above their Heart Chakra. This is balancing the head and the heart. What their head and heart want will be in sync. This is very relaxing and soothing.

11. *Hands over the Solar Plexus* – Move to the side of your recipient (either side is fine). Place your hands, one in front of the other, along the line of the diaphragm. You are directing energy to the Solar Plexus Chakra.

12. *Hands over the Navel* – Move your hands slightly lower so that they are over your recipient's navel. You are directing Reiki to the internal organs.

13. *Hands over the Sacral Chakra* – The easiest way to place your hands over your recipient's Sacral Chakra is to place one hand facing up the body (fingers pointing toward the head) and one hand facing down (fingertips pointing toward the feet).

14. *Hands on the knees* – Place one hand over each of your recipient's knees. It is a personal preference whether or not to have your hands touching the knees.

15. *Cup the soles of the feet* – As you cup the soles of your recipient's feet visualize tree roots of white light going from their feet into Mother Earth to ground them.

16. *Three aura sweeps* – Sweep the aura three times. Start two inches above your recipient and, using a sweeping motion, sweep the aura from head to foot to clear the Emotional Aura. Put the negative energy you collect into an imaginary bucket. Next do a sweep four inches above your recipient to clear the Mental Aura. Again put the negative energy into the imaginary bucket. Finally do a sweep six inches above your recipient to clear the Spiritual Aura. Put the negative energy into the imaginary bucket. Ask Mother Earth to transmute this negative energy into positive energy. Tilt the bucket of negative energy into Mother Earth for transmutation.

Hand Positions – Face Down

17. *Hands on the head* – If their head is turned, place one hand on the side and the other on the top.

18. *Back of the neck* – With your hands in a V-shape, place them over the back of your recipient's neck. This is the back of their Throat Chakra.

19. *Shoulders* – Place your hands a little lower to the top of your recipient's shoulders. It is a personal preference whether or not to have your hands touching the shoulders.

20. *Upper back* – Move to the side of your recipient (either side is fine). Place your hands, one in front of the other, along the back of their diaphragm. You are working on the Solar Plexus Chakra.

21. *Mid-back* – With your hands still one in front of the other, move to the mid-back. Here you are working on the back and the internal organs.

22. *Lower back* – With your hands still one in front of the other, move to the lower back. The lower back (back of the Sacral Chakra) is where we often store our worries about finances.

23. *Back of the knees* – Place your hands on the backs of your recipient's knees. You may have your hands touching the knees or not.

24. *Ankles* – Cup your recipient's ankles, one in each hand.

25. *Soles of the feet* – Cup the soles of their feet from the side or you may move to the bottom of your recipient. As you hold the soles of their feet, visualize tree roots of white light going from their feet into Mother Earth to ground them.

26. *Three aura sweeps* – Sweep the aura three times. Start two inches above your recipient and, using a sweeping motion, sweep the aura from head to foot to clear the Emotional Aura. Put the negative energy you collect into an imaginary bucket. Next do a sweep four inches above your recipient to clear the Mental Aura. Again put the negative energy into the imaginary bucket. Finally do a sweep six inches above your recipient to clear the Spiritual Aura. Put the negative energy into the imaginary bucket. Ask Mother Earth to transmute this negative energy into positive energy. Tilt the bucket of negative energy into Mother Earth for transmutation.

27. *Seal In the Reiki* – Send Reiki energy into each of your recipient's auras. Ask that the Reiki energy continue to flow to them after the session for as long as is needed.

28. Close the session by disconnecting your energy from that of your recipient. Ask for the white light to cover you and protect you. Place your hands back in prayer position in front of your Heart Chakra and thank your Reiki guides and Masters, spirit guides, and all other healers that helped you.

HAND POSITIONS — FACE UP

1. Protect yourself.
Call in your Reiki.

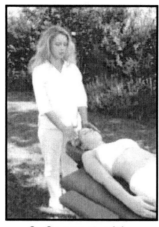

2. Connect with
your recipient.

3a. Roll their head to
place one hand
underneath.

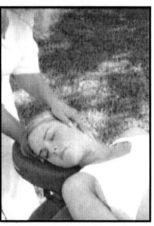

3b. Roll their head to
place other hand
underneath.

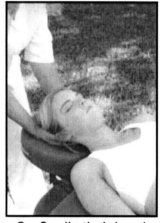

3c. Cradle their head
with both hands
underneath.

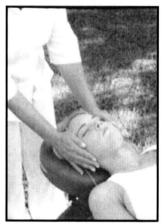

4. Hands over
the ears.

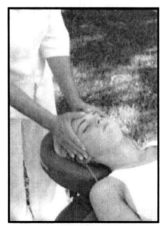

5. Thumbs over the
Third Eye

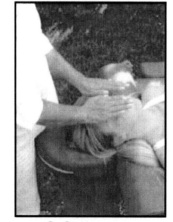

6. Cover eyes,
do not touch.

7. Throat Chakra

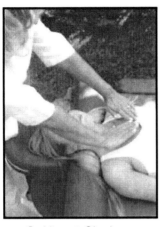

8. Heart Chakra

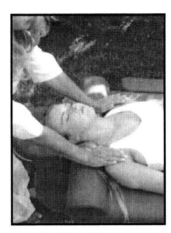

9. Shoulders

10. Balance head and heart

11. Solar Plexus Chakra

12. Navel

13. Sacral Chakra

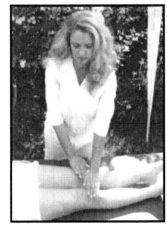

14. Knees

15. Soles of the feet. Grounding

Gail Thackray

16a. Aura sweep 1

16b. Aura sweep 2

16c. Aura sweep 3

HAND POSITIONS — FACE DOWN

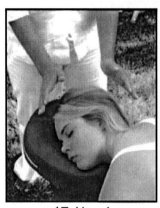

17. Head

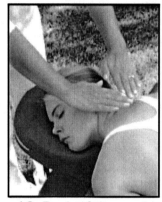

18. Back of the neck

19. Shoulders

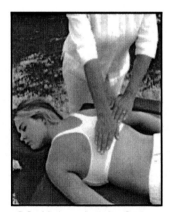

20. Upper back, Solar Plexus Chakra

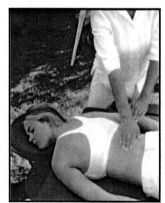

21. Mid-back

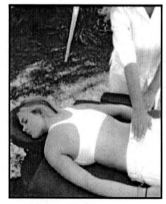

22. Lower back, Sacral Chakra

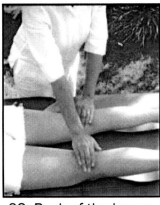
23. Back of the knees

24. Ankles

25. Soles of the feet.
Grounding

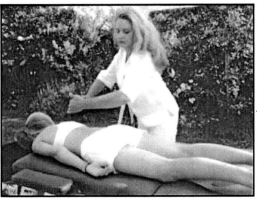
26a. Aura sweep 1

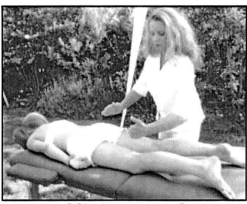
26b. Aura sweep 2

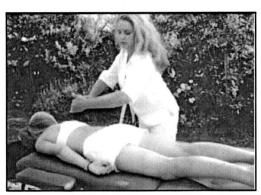
26c. Aura sweep 3

27. Seal In the Reiki

Close the session by disconnecting
your energy from that of your recipient.

CHAPTER 17

SPECIFIC AILMENTS

There are some wonderful reference books on illnesses and ailments where you can look up possible emotional causes or spiritual misalignments that may be the root cause of the physical problem. Some knowledge of this is invaluable and you will often find that as you pick up on such ailments in a Reiki session, they are related to an emotional or spiritual blockage in the person's life. Without going into great detail, here are some issues that I find repeat quite often.

The Right Side of the Body

The right side of the body is the more emotional/spiritual side. Ailments on the right side tend to have an emotional/spiritual root cause. For example, a pain in the right leg might indicate a reluctance to move forward, either in a spiritual manner or they are afraid to move forward on an emotional issue. The person might feel spiritually blocked or confused, like they've veered off their spiritual path or are having trouble connecting. Or it might be that they are not moving out of a difficult emotional situation that they know they need to resolve. For example, not addressing a relationship or situation that keeps them emotionally stuck, such as not leaving a bad relationship or allowing emotional abuse from someone.

The Left Side of the Body

The left side of the body is the more physical/practical side. Ailments on the left tend to have to do with physical or material issues. For example, a pain in the left leg might indicate a reluctance to move forward physically, such as changing jobs or moving homes.

CHAKRA IMBALANCES

I often find that if a chakra is out of balance, it represents certain emotional or spiritual misalignments that the person may be experiencing. If it has been left for too long, it could have manifested into a physical issue in that area. Vice versa, if someone complains of a specific condition, I often find that the chakra associated with that symptom may be blocked or slowed. Placing your hand over the chakra and sending Reiki will often clear up the physical symptom as well as the underlying emotional/spiritual issue that is causing the physical illness.

7th Chakra - Crown Chakra

- *Physical imbalance symptoms* – Headaches, confusion, dementia, depression, loneliness, insomnia.
- *Organ potentially affected* – Pineal gland
- *Possible underlying causes* – Fear of being alone, worry, loss of connection with spirituality, lack of trust (especially in God or a Higher Source).
- *Addressing the issues* – Send Reiki to the area and meditate, asking your Reiki guides to help you receive a stronger connection.

6th Chakra - Third Eye

- *Physical imbalance symptoms* – Headaches, sinus problems, eyesight issues, feeling blocked psychically, can't concentrate, insomnia, nightmares, feeling dizzy or spacey.
- *Organ potentially affected* – Pituitary gland
- *Possible underlying causes* – Don't want to look at something, turning a blind eye, avoiding a situation, being cynical.
- *Addressing the issues* – Send Reiki to the area and face your problems by looking at the situations. Do not ignore the signs.

5th Chakra - Throat Chakra

- *Physical imbalance symptoms* – Issues with the throat, neck, lungs, mouth, nose, or ears. Examples include sore throat, stuffy nose, thyroid issues, anorexia, bronchitis, earaches, mouth ulcers, speech issues, stiff neck, pinched nerve.

- *Organ potentially affected* – Thyroid

- *Possible underlying causes* – Not talking about something. Not feeling heard. Avoiding confrontation. Not speaking one's truth. Often couldn't speak up to parents or a spouse. Said something you regret. Telling lies that hurt someone.

- *Addressing the issues* – Send Reiki to the area. Stand up for yourself and be heard. If you can't talk to someone write them a letter. If you feel hurt by someone, send them love and forgiveness. Make sure you speak the truth. Don't talk negatively, only talk positively.

4th Chakra - Heart Chakra

- *Physical imbalance symptoms* – Heart issues, breast issues, immune system, circulation issues, allergies, sadness, depression.

- *Organs potentially affected* – Heart, thymus

- *Possible underlying causes* – Unresolved hurtful situations from romantic break-ups or family quarrels. Jealousy. Victim of insensitivity. Experienced lack of love.

- *Addressing the issues* – Send Reiki to your heart. Try to love yourself and allow yourself to experience unconditional love from God. Send white light and forgiveness to those who have hurt you.

3rd Chakra - Solar Plexus

- *Physical imbalance symptoms* – Issues with the liver, spleen, small intestine, stomach issues, ulcers, diabetes, gallstones. Feeling misunderstood by others. Blocks in career (the way others see you), stress and anxiety, shyness, irrational, feeling powerless, lacks confidence.

- *Organ potentially affected* – Pancreas

- *Possible underlying causes* – Unresolved guilt or anger, hate. Possible abuse of power by parents or teachers.

- *Addressing the issues* – Send Reiki to the area. Send white light and forgiveness to those who have hurt you.

2nd Chakra - Sacral Chakra

- *Physical imbalance symptoms* – Issues with the uterus, fibroids, menstrual cycle, PMS, prostate, large intestine, bladder.

- *Organ potentially affected* – Ovaries or testicles

- *Possible underlying causes* – Possessiveness, jealousy, relationship/romantic issues, holding resentment, victim of sexual abuse.

- *Addressing the issues* – Send Reiki to the area. Send white light and forgiveness to those who have hurt you. Never use words like, "he is a pain in the neck," which can manifest neck pain.

2nd Chakra - Sacral Chakra - Back

- *Physical imbalance symptoms* – Lower back issues

- *Possible underlying causes* – Worrying about finances, mistrust of the universal supply. Feeling like you are burdened with financially supporting others.

- *Addressing the issues* – Send Reiki to the area. Believe in God as your never-ending supply of all that you need and desire.

1st Chakra - Base Chakra

- **Physical imbalance symptoms** – Issues with bladder, kidneys, lower intestines, constipation, IBS, hemorrhoids, cold fingers and toes, spinal column, sciatic nerves, feeling unbalanced.

- **Organ potentially affected** – Adrenals

- **Possible underlying causes** – Fear, lack of stability, feeling weak, issues with family support, feeling like you can't find your life's purpose. Often unresolved early childhood issues.

- **Addressing the issues** – Send Reiki to the area. Send white light and forgiveness to those who have hurt you. Meditate on painful childhood memories and ask your guides to help you release these.

PHYSICAL MANIFESTATIONS – AREA SPECIFIC

Knees

- **Physical symptoms** – Physical issues with knees, ankles and legs.

- **Possible underlying causes** – Being stubborn, need to be more flexible.

- **Addressing the issues** – Send Reiki to the area. Look at areas in your life where you need to be more flexible.

Legs and Hips

- **Physical symptoms** – Physical issues with legs and hips.

- **Possible underlying causes** – Being reluctant to move forward (left side - a physical/material world move, right side - an emotional move).

- **Addressing the issues** – Send Reiki to the area. Look at areas in your life where you feel stuck or scared to move on even though you know it is the right thing. Take a leap of faith.

Back

- See Sacral Chakra above

Shoulders

- *Physical Symptoms* – Tension in the shoulders and upper back.

- *Possible underlying causes* – Feeling like you are the emotional support for many people. Family emotional issues.

- *Addressing the issues* – Send Reiki to the area. Make sure you allow your loved ones to support themselves. Love and nurture yourself more.

Skin Issues

- *Physical symptoms* – Allergies, skin rashes, dry skin.

- *Possible underlying causes* – Feeling like you are uncomfortable in your own skin. Severe lack of confidence, feeling not worthy.

- *Addressing the issues* – Meditate and ask your Reiki guides to put a layer of Reiki over your body. Charge your creams and oils with Reiki before you apply them. Meditate with your Reiki guides on your purpose in life. Send love to those who have hurt you.

CHAPTER 18

PENDULUMS

What is a Pendulum?

Basically any weight on the end of a string or chain will act as a pendulum. You can also find beautiful ones made of gemstones, crystals, or metals (e.g. copper). The pendulum carries the energy of the material or particular crystal that it is made from. Pendulums come in different shapes. The most common is the traditional cone shape with a point at the end. Egyptian pendulums are more elongated and can have distinctive geometric forms. Other shapes may include round balls or star-shaped (Merkaba).

Uses of the Pendulum

The pendulum dates back thousands of years. It is thought that the pendulum was first used for the art of dowsing to locate underground water sources, minerals, and precious metals, as well as to divine answers. Now it is mostly used in natural healing, to test chakras, and for divination.

> A pendulum is most reliable for determining health issues or energy imbalances.

How to Use Your Pendulum

To use your pendulum, follow these simple instructions:

Before You Start

- Always protect yourself with Divine white light as you would with any connection to Spirit.

- Ask if you have a spirit from the white light working through your pendulum (instructions on how to find your YES sign are below).

Asking Yes/No Questions

- To begin you will want your pendulum to be in the resting position. This means that it is simply hanging straight down and stationary (as you hold it by the end of its chain). To do this, take a deep breath, relax your mind, clear your thoughts, and just allow the pendulum to stop (be still). You will want to do this before you ask each question in order to get a clear response.

- You are now going to determine your specific directions for YES/NO answers. These directions are unique to each person. As you allow the pendulum to hang freely, say, "Give me the direction for a 'Yes' answer." Your pendulum will start to swing. (It may take a moment to start moving.) It may swing back and forth, side to side, or rotate in a circle (either clockwise or counterclockwise). This direction, once established, is now your "Yes" answer. This will be your "Yes" direction for any pendulum you use. Now use the same method to find your "No" direction. Ask it to give you the "No" direction and note the motion. Once you have determined the motion of your answers, you may begin.

- For each answer, the pendulum will either move in a circle (clockwise or counterclockwise) or a straight line (vertical or horizontal). Each individual will establish their own unique direction. This direction will now be your signal for YES or NO with any pendulum you use.

- You may use your pendulum during a Reiki session to ask yes or no questions about your recipient's health or other concerns. Such as, "Is this energy imbalance an effect of her current relationship?"

- When choosing a pendulum you can ask, "Is this a good pendulum for me to work with?"

- If you are having difficulty, such as the pendulum bobbing up and down, but not going in a particular direction, try changing the wording of your question to be more specific.

- When starting a session and asking questions to your pendulum, start by confirming, "Do I have a spirit from the white light that is working with me through this pendulum?"

- You can overdo the yes or no pendulum questions by continuing to ask in different ways until you get the answer you want. At this point you will not get accurate answers. Also, if you are too emotionally involved in the answer this may affect the accuracy. In this case, you may want to have another person ask the questions. Alternatively, you can write the possible answers on pieces of paper, turn the papers facedown, and mix them up. Then ask your pendulum, "Is this the answer?"

To Detect Energy Imbalances

I find that a pendulum is most reliable for determining health issues or energy imbalances.

- If you are in the middle of a Reiki session you will have already protected yourself with white light. If not and you are just starting a connection with spirit, ask for white light of protection.

- Hold the pendulum over each of your recipient's chakras. You may do this in turn, starting at the Crown Chakra and moving down to the Base Chakra. If your recipient is lying down, place the pendulum about four inches above the top of the head. (Remember, since they are lying down, this position isn't above the front of the head, but rather a few inches out past the top of their head). For the other chakras, hold the pendulum about two inches above the body. For the Base Chakra, you do not want to place the pendulum between their legs. Place the pendulum about four to six inches below the groin area and about two inches above the thighs. Have the intention that the pendulum pick up on the energy of the Base Chakra.

- You do not need to do this in order, you can simply check one chakra if you feel you need some guidance on the energy of that chakra and then continue your Reiki session.

- The pendulum acts like a magnet, showing the electric field of the chakra and will rotate at the same speed and direction as the person's chakra. If it is slow, it means that the chakra is slow or slightly shut down. If it is stopped, the chakra is completely shut down. If it bounces up and down or is choppy, this is an energy imbalance. Applying Reiki should clear and open the chakra and then you can retest it. A healthy chakra should rotate at an even energetic pace, smoothly in one direction.

- After checking the chakras on one side, ask your recipient to turn over and recheck them on the other side. The chakras should rotate in the opposite direction as you are now looking at the backside of the chakra.

- The direction of the chakra is individual to each person. Some people's chakras rotate clockwise, other people's rotate counterclockwise, and some have a mixture of the two (meaning a person can have some of their chakras rotate one direction while others in the opposite direction). As long as they are rotating smoothly and with good speed, they are perfectly healthy.

- The pendulum is not healing or in anyway affecting the energy imbalances. It simply acts as a guide to tell you where to direct your Reiki energy.

- You can test your own chakras, although it is a little more difficult to hold the pendulum above your own body. You can also check the chakras in your palms. We have small chakras in the center of each palm. It is interesting to check your palm chakras first and then "power up" your Reiki energy and then re-check your palm chakras. You will probably see that the energy increases.

Note:

If you are having difficulty getting a clear YES/NO or finding the energy vortex (chakra), make sure you have asked for protection and have confirmed that a spirit from the white light is working with you. You can also cleanse your pendulum by burning sage and letting the smoke run over it or placing the pendulum in a bowl of water with sea salt.

CHAPTER 19

USING REIKI

Can You Pass Negative Reiki?

Reiki is never negative. That is like saying can you pass negative white light. It is not affected by the person who is being used as the channel. Therefore you cannot get "bad" Reiki from anyone. It is not dependant on the sender as it is not coming from the sender, but rather it is flowing through them. At the very worst, the Reiki energy will have to work harder to get through to the recipient if it has to first heal the sender, but never be afraid of receiving or sending bad Reiki. There is no such thing.

Reiki Cannot Be Forced on Someone

You should only send Reiki to a person who has requested it or that you have asked first. However, you cannot force Reiki to someone regardless. A person will only receive it if their higher self allows it. If you cannot request permission (i.e. the person is too young or too sick), just ask that their higher self receive it if it is the person's highest and best interest.

You can never give a person too much Reiki.

You Don't Need to Believe

Even if a person does not believe in the effects of Reiki but has given permission for you to send them Reiki, it can still work. A person does not have to believe in it in order for it to work. The person's higher self will receive it, if it chooses.

Does Everyone Get Cured?

Not everyone is healed with Reiki. Some people report miraculous cures from Reiki but others don't. Sometimes the purpose of sending Reiki is not to heal them but to help a person pass more comfortably to the other side. Sometime the purpose of Reiki is to open a person spiritually but not to heal them physically.

What About Karma?

There arises a question as to whether we interfere with a person's karma if we provide Reiki and heal them. Using Reiki can assist the person's higher self in releasing and dissolving karmic issues if it is in their highest good. But Reiki never interferes with a person's karma.

Too Much or Too Little Reiki

You can never give a person too much Reiki because there are no negative side effects. If you have limited time, giving a short session is better than none at all, and the Reiki guides once connected can continue their work, even after you have finished the session.

Reiki Instead of Medical Treatment

Never suggest to a person that they replace or reject medical treatment. Reiki is not a substitute for medical intervention. However, Reiki may work well in conjunction with a medical doctor's prescribed treatment. For example, Reiki energy may help the medication work better or aid the healing process in conjunction with the existing medical treatment. Never diagnose. You may pass on messages from Spirit, but always encourage the person to seek medical attention for any suspected illness.

Can I Catch or Pass an Illness?

If a person has a contagious illness such as the flu or a cold, clearly this can be passed from one to another just by being in the same room. Although it is somewhat limited since there is no skin on skin contact. Use your common sense. As far as receiving psychic ailments, you are protecting yourself with white light and are running Reiki energy through you, and thus are much more protected than if you were just sitting next to that person.

Is It Ok After a Glass of Wine?

You should never give a Reiki session after consuming any alcohol. The same goes for connecting in any manner to the spirit world. You do not want to impair your protection and encourage any negative spirits. If you give Reiki to a person who has consumed alcohol, there is no risk of breaking your own protection. However, the Reiki energy will process the effects more quickly and your recipient can go from a happy buzz straight to a hangover very quickly!

CHAPTER 20

OTHER USES OF REIKI

Healing Small Children

Reiki can be used on babies and small children. You may not be able to do the specific hand positions so just improvise and use your intuition. You can even do Reiki on a baby in utero by working on the pregnant mother. Reiki is perfectly safe and cannot harm a baby or child. Children and babies have not yet built up blocks or negative ideas about Reiki and will absorb the energy quickly and easily.

Healing Animals

Animals are much more open spiritually than we are. They are already communicating with us, even if we are not aware of it. Animals love Reiki and will often come around when you are giving a Reiki session. An animal also knows when they have received enough and may get up and walk away when they feel the session is complete.

Healing Plants

Use Reiki to help your plants grow healthy and fruitful. It has been documented that plants respond to being "talked to" in a positive way. They also absorb Reiki energy easily. You can use it to help a failing plant or help the growth of a seedling. Reiki is especially good to do on plants that bear fruits and vegetables you plan to harvest.

Bless your food with Reiki before meals.

Blessing Water

Dr. Masaru Emoto, author of "Hidden Messages In Water," discovered that molecules of water are impacted by our thoughts. Similarly, Reiki has a very positive impact on water. Blessing the water that we drink or even bathe in sets a more positive energy to the water we consume. Being that a significant percentage of the human body is water, this can have quite an impact.

Blessing Food

Try doing Reiki on your food before meals. You can also do Reiki during the harvest, selection, and preparation of your food. You are a reflection of what you eat. Bless your food and provide your body with spiritual nutrition as well. You will notice that not only do you feel healthier, but your food tastes better as well.

Blessing Medicines and Vitamins

Reiki is never a substitute for medical intervention. In fact, the spirits and Reiki energy know if you are receiving medical treatment and the energy will work in conjunction with your medical treatment. Therefore, why not give a Reiki blessing to the medicines you are receiving? This also applies to any natural medicines, vitamins, or other supplements you are taking.

Blessing Objects

You can bless any object with Reiki. Bless gifts before you give them. Bless the candles you light, the flowers you place around your home, or the paperwork for your meeting. Be creative. You can bless any object.

CHAPTER 21

REIKI WITH OTHER MODALITIES

Reiki works very well in conjunction with other therapies or modalities.

Massage

Reiki energy can become part of your massage sessions. You could prepare your room with the Reiki energy. During the massage, you may call in your Reiki energy and then do your massage therapy as usual with enhanced energy hands. Or you could do Reiki on your client either before or at the end of the massage. Use your guidance as to what feels best for you.

Reflexology

This is the art of light massage on the soles of the feet or sometime the hands. Prepare your space and call in the Reiki energy, asking it to flow and guide you during the reflexology session.

Crystal Chakra Clearing

In a crystal therapy session, the practitioner will usually place certain types of crystal beads or crystal pieces over the various chakras to aid, balance, and rejuvenate them. When adding Reiki, place the crystals as you would normally for a crystal session and then leave them in place as you complete a Reiki session. When you ask

> Reiki works well with massage, reflexology, crystals, homeopathy, hypnosis, divination, and other modalities.

your client to turn over to do Reiki on their backside, remove and then place the crystals again after they have flipped. Continue with your Reiki session.

Homeopathy, Herbs, Essential Oils

If you are working with homeopathic remedies, herbs, essential oils, or other supplements, you can infuse them with Reiki energy. Send Reiki energy to the remedy, asking your Reiki guides and Masters to bless and empower it. If you bless the whole bottle, all of the contents will remain charged with this Reiki energy. Your Reiki guides can also help you in your selection of natural remedies. For example, which essential oil to use during a Reiki session and where to place it. Ask your guides how to work best with your modality.

Hypnosis

Reiki can be used during a hypnosis or past life regression session. For example, you may want to prepare your room using Reiki energy and ask your Reiki guides to help you conduct your hypnosis session. Perhaps you may start with a Reiki hands-on session and then go into your hypnosis work during the session while your recipient is relaxed and receiving Reiki.

Divination

Reiki can be added to the divination arts, such as using cards (Tarot, Angel, or other divination cards). First protect yourself and call in your Reiki energy. Ask your Reiki guides to give you guidance in regard to your question. Then ask them to help you select the appropriate card and to give you the intuition you need to interpret it. Perhaps you can ask your Reiki guides to send Reiki to the situation or guidance that you are being given.

These are only a few suggestions. Ask your Reiki guides how you can incorporate Reiki into other modalities that you use.

CHAPTER 22

USING CRYSTALS WITH REIKI

Crystals and Continuous Healing

Working with crystals in conjunction with Reiki healing works very well. Each type of crystal or gemstone has specific properties and energies. For example, amethyst is known to help with your connection to the spirit world, the other side. Turquoise stones such as larimar resonate with the Throat Chakra and are wonderful for communication.

It is not the power of the crystal alone that imparts these benefits. Although the crystal is a vessel for holding certain energies or intentions and for perpetuating these energies, the real key is for the practitioner to first charge the crystal with their healing intention so that the crystal can hold and amplify this energy. Do not expect the crystal to do all the work for you without charging it with your intention fist.

If you charge crystals with your intention, they will hold the Reiki energy and perpetuate and enhance your intention.

Intention is foremost in Reiki. As long as your intention is clear, your guides can work through you even if you do not perform your Reiki session exactly to the ritual that you have learned. The same is true for crystals. If you first charge them with your intention they will hold the Reiki energy and perpetuate and enhance the intention that you have stated. It helps to choose an appropriate crystal or stone that is most aligned with the energy of your intention.

Clear quartz crystals are the most universal and widely used crystals as the pure quartz can hold and absorb your thoughts and intention for all purposes. A clear quartz crystal can be used for any kind of healing, manifesting, or Reiki session. It can also be used as a substitute for any other stone.

To charge the crystal, call in the Reiki energy just as you would before a hands-on healing session. Then state your intention and ask for the Reiki to flow from your hands. Now place your hands around the crystal to charge your crystal with Reiki and the intention that you desire, whether just to send positive Reiki through the session or a specific healing.

Using Crystals During a Session

You may use crystals during your Reiki hands-on healing sessions. Though you should be familiar enough with crystals and crystal healing before you start to incorporate them into your sessions. Some crystal healing practitioners place the crystal directly on the chakra. A crystal is chosen for each chakra that holds the type of energy vibration that is desired for that chakra. That is, they may choose a rose quartz to lay on the Heart Chakra and a string of turquoise beads to lay on the Throat Chakra. It may help to use stones on a string, a large flat stone, or stones inside a pouch so that the crystals can rest on your client without falling off if the client moves slightly. Some crystal workers believe placing a crystal directly on the chakra has an energy that is too strong and recommend not to. I personally have never seen any adverse reaction to using crystals directly on the chakras.

More often you will be using crystals to energize and purify your room. You may place crystals around your room or under your massage table with the intention of holding and transmitting Reiki energy as you perform your session.

Cleansing Your Crystals

After you have chosen a crystal, or in some cases the crystal has chosen you, it is necessary to cleanse the crystal of any inappropriate energy or simply of the energy it has absorbed from yourself or others. To cleanse a crystal you can use any of the following methods:

1. Place the crystal in a bowl of rock or sea salt, making sure it is completely covered. If you can leave it overnight, especially under a full moon, that would be great but not necessary.

2. Use salt water. Add sea salt to a bowl of water, usually about a teaspoon to a tablespoon of salt depending on the size of the bowl. Be sure to use enough water to completely submerge the crystals.

3. Do Reiki over the crystal asking for it to be cleansed.

4. Place your crystal under running water. I place my crystals in my fresh water stream but if you don't have access to a natural water source, then you can use running water from your sink or tap.

5. If you live by the ocean you can cleanse them in the sea. Just make sure to have a good hold of them or place them in a mesh bag so you don't lose them to the tide.

6. Smudge the crystal with sage smoke.

7. Place them in a bowl of holy water.

Do whichever of these cleansing methods feels right to you. You will want to do a quick cleanse between any treatments, even self-treatments. Native Americans believe that you should leave your crystals in red cotton or felt when they are not being used.

Charging Your Crystals

After you have cleansed your crystal, you may now charge it with Reiki. One way of charging a crystal is to let it sit in the sunlight. You may want to give it a sun charge before you start your Reiki charge.

To charge it with Reiki:

1. Protect yourself psychically and call in your Reiki energy.

2. Hold the crystal between your hands and send Reiki energy to it, intending that the crystal will be charged.

3. Include a prayer asking that your Reiki guides and Masters bless your crystal.

    State your intention to help and to heal other through its use or if there is a more specific intention, state that now.

CHAPTER 23

ANIMAL REIKI

Animals are particularly receptive to receiving Reiki. They have not created the blockages or the disbelief/doubts that we have. Animals are already very spiritually advanced and able to tap into the universal consciousness. They communicate telepathically and hear and understand on a spiritual level much more than we know. They are mostly healers themselves and are quite adept at aligning their own energy and receiving healing from Spirit. They love to receive Reiki.

Animals are Healers

Our animals often mimic our health issues. For instance, if you have a bad leg, your dog may start to limp. This is partly because they want to make us aware of our own health problems and address them. It is also because they come around us and absorb our negative emotions and issues as a form of healing to us. Normally they can process and remove this energy pretty easily. As they get older or if the energy becomes too much, they, too, can develop health issues. So in a way, we can cause some of our pet's issues but don't feel bad. Our animals love us unconditionally and are more than happy to help us. We can help them by giving them regular Reiki, not just for their health issues, but to keep them in tune and clear of our negative thoughts and emotions.

Doing an Animal Reiki Session

Animals have the same chakras as we do. Their exact location varies slightly due to the shape of the animal but it is approximately the same. If you can, prepare the room or area as you would for a Reiki session. Protect yourself and call in your Reiki. You can try to adapt the hand positions for your pet. Sometimes it is hard to get them to sit still. You can also hold them. Do what is comfortable for them. Ask your Reiki to flow and to go where it is needed. Even if the animal will just allow you only a couple of minutes, it's better than none at all and you can ask your Reiki guides to continue working on them after. Another method you can try is to call in your Reiki and use it as you would normally stroke or pet the animal so they don't feel alarmed. For wild animals or very timid animals, hand positions are more difficult. At Reiki level II, you will learn how to send Reiki at a distance. This is very useful for treating animals, especially those who cannot be handled or won't be still enough for a hands-on session.

Infusing their Food and Other Items

Reiki can be used in many different ways for your pet. Empower your pet's food, water, or medicine with Reiki and bless objects such as their bed or collar. You can also charge a stone or crystal pendant to use as a charm on their collar (just make sure it is safe to not tangle or get caught). Another way to add this energy is to charge a crystal with Reiki and place it by their food bowl or where they sleep.

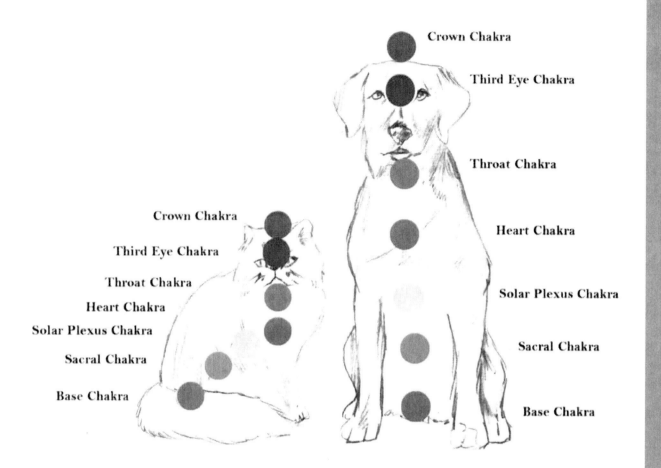

Crown Chakra

Third Eye Chakra

Throat Chakra

Heart Chakra

Solar Plexus Chakra

Sacral Chakra

Base Chakra

Crown Chakra

Third Eye Chakra

Throat Chakra

Heart Chakra

Solar Plexus Chakra

Sacral Chakra

Base Chakra

CHAPTER 24
MEDITATION

In the five ideals of Reiki, Dr. Usui emphasizes the importance of daily meditation. Meditation doesn't mean you have to go into some kind of trance or zoned-out state. It can simply mean a quiet relaxed time, a time of reverence.

Try to take at least a few minutes each day to just sit, relax, and talk to your inner self. Connect with your guides and rejuvenate your spiritual body. Your state of mind has much to do with your ability to accomplish goals, manifest what you want in your life, and deal with day-to-day challenges. Being in a restful state of mind is a necessity if you want to achieve the best results.

Sometimes we get too caught up in our day-to-day life, dealing with stressful situations, and coming from a place of reaction instead of acceptance Meditation is an important tool that allows you to know that you are not alone; that you are divinely guided. It helps you to be in a place of understanding the bigger picture.

If you can meditate for a half an hour every morning or for a specific allotted time during the day, the benefits that you receive will bring you more than the time you have spent.

Some people can easily slip in to a meditative state and don't need a structured meditation. Others prefer having a meditation "tool" or detailed framework to connect them and give them a direction.

Here is a structured meditation that you may want to try for asking a question, to prepare yourself to give a session, or to charge a crystal or object with Reiki.

REIKI MEDITATION

Centering Yourself Through Reiki

1. Find a quiet place where you will not be disturbed. Turn off the phone and remove yourself from all distractions. Sit comfortably with your feet uncrossed and firmly planted on Mother Earth. Place your palms face-up on your lap.

2. Concentrating on your breathing, breathing slow deep breaths. Breath in positive energy through your nose into your diaphragm and release all the negativity as you exhale through your mouth.

3. Imagine a white ball of light coming down from the sky, hovering over your Third Eye and then spreading its energy over your body, covering you and protecting you in a bubble of white light.

4. Imagine tree roots of white light coming out from the soles of your feet and going into Mother Earth, completely grounding you.

5. Tap your crown and call in your Reiki energy. Then tap each of your palms three times and ask for the energy to flow.

6. Imaging the Reiki energy spreading out through your entire body, healing and energizing as it expands.

7. Now you are charged with Reiki energy and ready to concentrate on any question or goal that you have and to communicate directly with your guides.

8. Take each question you have individually. Contemplate the question. Ask your Reiki guides and Masters for advice and see what intuitions you receive.

9. Take each goal and visualize that goal happening in a perfect way. You may say an affirmation such as, "May this come to pass immediately and in perfect ways, in my highest of goodness." Visualize a ball of white light encapsulating your goal.

   (Or this is where you would state the intention to prepare you to give a Reiki session, or to charge your crystal or an object with Reiki.)

10. As you finish and prepare to come back, re-imagine the tree roots of white light going down into Mother Earth to ground you. Start to become aware of your physical body; your feet on the ground and your bottom on the chair.

11. **Slowly bring** yourself back to your physical existence and slowly open your eyes.

12. **Thank your** Reiki guides and Masters for working with you.

CHAPTER 25

WHAT TO EXPECT IN A REIKI WORKSHOP

Reiki workshops vary quite a bit from Reiki Master to Reiki Master. All must include an attunement to the specific level of Reiki being taught. However, there can still be great diversity of instruction. Some Reiki Masters teach a very short course that may consist of the history of Reiki, the hand positions, and the attunement. Other Masters incorporate many of their personal insights, in-depth discussion, and practice sessions. One of my students came to retake her Reiki levels with me because her first Reiki teacher only gave her the attunements and then told her to go buy any Reiki book to figure out the rest!

It is the attunement itself that is truly the most important part of the course. Some Masters prefer to give attunements one at a time. Others take large groups and give the attunements very quickly. All of this works. If you have been attuned by a certified Reiki Master, your Reiki channel is open and the Reiki energy will flow through you. Whether your Master teaches you the hand positions or gives you a book, it doesn't matter. Once you have been attuned, your Reiki journey has begun and you have been given the power that you need to proceed. What you ultimately do with it is up to you.

The following is an overview of what one of my Reiki level I workshops might consist of, so you can visualize yourself going through the course with me or you can use this to create your own experience.

Sample Reiki Level I Workshop

Here's an example of one of my Reiki Level I workshops. It is a full day, lasting approximately six hours.

REIKI LEVEL I - SCHEDULE

12:00	Introduction, meet and greet
12:15	Meet your Reiki guide meditation
12:30	Angel blessings
12:45	Reiki manual – discussion and excerpts, passing energy
1:30	Gratitude walk, collect stones
2:00	Attunement preparation
2:15	ATTUNEMENTS (Students will be attuned individually) Lunch, reflection cards, personal reflection/meditation
3:30	Self-healing tutorial, hand positions
4:00	Practice sessions (giving and receiving)
5:00	How to use a pendulum, clearing chakras
5:30	Crystals and other healing modalities
5:45	Closing
6:00	Certificates

Meet and Greet

Before the workshop, I send out Reiki preparation instructions. These instructions include meditation in preparation for your Reiki journey, as well as dietary suggestions to clear your energetic field. There is guidance for those who wish to fast, cleanse, or at least limit their dietary consumption before their attunement. Some people choose to do a three-day fast, some for just a day. Others don't fast at all. It's a personal choice.

When people arrive for the workshop, I try not to tempt the fasting ones and put out only water and decaffeinated teas. When it is time for the attunements, I attune the fasting ones first so that they can begin their lunch first.

I like to begin by having everyone introduce themselves and talk about how they discovered Reiki. I find that my workshops include people from all walks of life. Some have no background in healing and this is their first introduction to spirituality. Others are professional psychics and healers that wish to add Reiki to the services they offer. With each group, I find that there becomes a common bond and these people often stay connected and continue to grow spiritually together.

I provide each student with a manual as well as a small gift. My gift may consist of a purple candle on a non-flammable dish as well as some herbs and sage that grow at my ranch.

My Introduction

I open by telling my students how I got started on my Reiki journey and how it has changed my life. I also discuss the basics of what Reiki is and what to expect today.

Meet Your Reiki Guide

I next lead my students on a guided meditation to meet their Reiki guides. (This meditation is in Chapter 7, page 28). I begin by guiding them through how to protect, which should be done before any spiritual work. We then begin the meditation. Since the Reiki guides already know that their person is coming to the workshop, they are always there, ready for their person to be attuned, as well as excited to begin working with them. Students are often surprised that they are able to sense or see details of their guides.

Angel Blessing

I pass out an angel blessing card to each person at the beginning of the day. Often these blessings turn out to have a very pertinent message. At the end of the day we check back on our blessings, and oftentimes these messages have shown to be surprisingly relevant.

The Reiki Manual

I do a short run-through of the manual. I share the history of Reiki, stories of Dr. Usui, the basic principles and ideals of Reiki, and how to use Reiki. The different levels of Reiki are introduced, as well as chakras, auras, and other concepts that we are going to be using. We also discuss the beginning of your Reiki journey.

Passing Energy

Even before having had a Reiki attunement, we all sense, to a certain degree, feelings and energies, and can pass energy from one to another. To demonstrate this and show that we already have this ability, we do an exercise of passing energy. The students pair up and decide who is going to be the receiver and who is going to be the sender. The sender is then guided that they are going to be sending the feeling of love. They are asked to put this feeling into the form of a shape, giving this shape a color and smell. They are to imagine this shape and its attributes, and then choose an animal to pass it and this love to the receiver. However, they do not tell the receiver any of this information. The receiver is going to try to energetically sense the shape, its attributes, and the animal that is being sent. The receiver is simply to allow the waves of messages and feelings to pass over them and then to share what they receive. The partners then switch, so each person can experience both sending and receiving.

It is always amazing how many people are able to sense many of the aspects of the energy that is being sent. Some of the receivers are able to describe the shape and its attributes nearly completely. I've even seen senders pick a color and then switch it in their mind just as they are sending it, and the recipient picks up on both colors!

Gratitude Walk

This is probably my favorite part of the day. I live on a ranch and am blessed to be able to include nature in my workshops. I teach the workshop outdoors and include a trip to my stream on the gratitude walk.

As we walk to the stream, I ask my students to think about nature and to be grateful for the beautiful nature around us, really noticing and appreciating the flowers, trees and the little animals. I then ask them to think about what they are grateful for in their lives, their family, their work, and their ability to be here today. I instruct everyone that whenever negative thoughts creep in, like "I am grateful for my teenager but I just wish they would listen to me..." that they immediately override it with a positive thought.

I take my students to a very picturesque spot at the stream where the water cascades over a small waterfall. The riverbed is filled with pebbles and stones. I instruct my students to choose 21 stones from the river. The 21 stones represent the 21 stones that Dr. Usui used on his retreat in the mountains to count out his 21 days. Everyone then takes a moment at the riverbed to contemplate their lives and what they are grateful for, while listening to the soothing sounds of the waterfall. I take each student's stones. First I cleanse them under the running waterfall and then charge them with my Reiki energy before giving them back to the student.

I bless and send Reiki to Mother Earth as I have taken these stone from her. I also scatter seeds to thank Mother Earth. It is a Native American tradition to give something back when you take a stone, a feather, or some object from the land. This is a tradition that I like and honor.

These are the 21 stones that my students will use to count out the 21 self-healing sessions they will do. I instruct them to place a Reiki candle and dish by their bed and to lay the stones on the dish. Then, as they do each self-healing session, take one stone away and put it in another container. When all the stones are gone, the student has finished their 21 self-healing treatments. This is an easy way to keep track of how many healings have been done, especially if the sessions are not always done on consecutive nights.

On the way back from the river, the students are asked to be grateful for something they wish to receive in their lives. I tell them to feel grateful as if it were already theirs because it is already on the psychic plane waiting to manifest for them.

We also collect different types of sage, rosemary, lavender, and lemon verbena that I am lucky to have growing on the ranch. The sage we will use for smudging and the herbs to give nice atmosphere to our Reiki sessions.

Preparing for the Attunement

I like to explain exactly what is going to happen during the attunement. I tell everyone that each person will be doing a private attunement with me and let them know how they'll be seated and how to place their hands. I also explain what it may feel like and what to expect. Some Reiki Masters like to keep their students in the dark about what is happening. I think students get more out of it if they can understand what is going on.

Receiving the Attunement

The student is seated in a chair starting with their hands in the prayer position. I instruct the student to concentrate on the energy coming from their Reiki guides and Masters in spirit who are going to be working with them. Then I proceed with the attunement. During the attunement, I will gently squeeze the student's shoulder when I want them to raise their hands above their Crown Chakra. The student keeps their eyes closed during the attunement and my chants are done silently so the student may not be aware of what is happening. Usually the student will feel the energy as a heat or light sensation, or a tingling through their body. They may feel energized and sometimes a little disorientated.

Blessing Mother Earth

While I am attuning a student, the others have assignments to do. Their first Reiki assignment after their attunement is to practice sending Reiki to Mother Earth. They are to go outside and choose a flower, a plant, or just the ground. Then they call in their Reiki guides and Masters and ask the Reiki energy to flow. The student then places their hands just above the plant or the ground and sends Reiki energy.

Reflection Cards

Another assignment is to use Reiki while asking a question using my reflection card deck. The student calls in their Reiki guides and Masters in spirit and asks them a question. The student then chooses a reflection card. The card chosen is their Reiki guide's answer to their question.

Self-Healing

It is important that we learn to heal ourselves first, as this allows us to be a clearer and therefore stronger channel. We learn the self-healing hand positions and I guide my students through a self-healing session. We hold each position for just a few minutes or however long we feel is necessary. I explain to my students that the hand positions do not have to be exact and that what is most important is their intention. We practice doing the self-healing hand positions both sitting and lying down. This is the first of our 21 self-healing sessions that we need to complete.

Practice Sessions

This is the part everyone has been waiting for. We partner up to do practice hands-on Reiki sessions. Each student gets the opportunity to both send and receive. I usually face the Reiki beds so that the students can see me and I guide them through an example of a hands-on session. The recipient simply enjoys the experience. I then have the partners discuss it so that the receiver can share what they felt and the sender can explain what they sensed. Most of the time students are surprised at what they pick up and the receiver often feels strong energy.

Pendulums

We learn how to use pendulums for yes/no questions and for detecting the chakras. Now we repeat the practice session, this time incorporating the pendulum to check the chakras.

Crystals

We discuss the energy of crystals and their use in Reiki. We may also do a mini practice session using crystals.

Other Notes

We discuss the many uses of Reiki and how it can be incorporated into other modalities that the students may be practicing or would like to learn. This is a great time for any other questions and final discussions.

Closing

I issue the certificates on the same day. It is up to the student to do their 21 days of self-healing and then to start using this beautiful energy.

CHAPTER 26

SPREADING THE WORD

I believe Reiki is meant to be shared with the world. If everyone could live their day-to-day lives based on the principles and ethics of Reiki, the world would be a much better place.

It is now time to go out and explore your connection to this Reiki energy. If you believe you are benefiting from this energy you may want to consider going on to Level II and becoming a Reiki practitioner, either professionally or just for your own spiritual development.

I really hope you will enjoy the Reiki journey and that you will bring this into your life and spread the word to many others.

ACKNOWLEDGMENTS

Your Reiki journey is not completing; rather it has just begun. As you travel down this path, I hope you will research, read, learn, and experience from the many works of those that spread the word of Reiki, as well as meet many other Reiki practitioners.

Just as you continue your Reiki search, so do I. It is from this continuous journey that I have collected the many truths contained here. Some information here has been passed down from my Auntie Pauline and her Masters. Some has been gathered from my continual Reiki search. Some has been Divinely guided. I have endeavored to provide you with all the elements of the traditional Reiki Usui system, level I, as well as other material I present here for your consideration on your Reiki path.

Therefore my first and very special thanks goes to my auntie:
Reiki Master, **Pauline Landy**

For without Pauline, I may never have been introduced to this wonderful energy and, through this, my connection to Source, which has lit the spiritual path of my life.

And to her son:
Reiki Master, **Ric Landy**

Who continues to support and inspire me on my Reiki journey.

Additionally, I would like to thank the Masters in my Reiki lineage who have contributed to my attunement and to those Masters who spread the word and knowledge through their devotion to teaching and authoring on Reiki. In particular:
Pat Hudson, William Rand, Simon Treselyan, and John Watson

And of course for the lineage of Reiki itself:

Mikao Usui, Chujiro Hayashi and Hawayo Takata

And all my Reiki Masters and Guides in spirit

With thanks for the support of my family, friends, assistants, and Reiki students who have helped and supported me in my teaching, particularly: **my mom** and **my daughters,** and my Reiki Master students, **Donna, Vicky, Robert** and **Cindy.** And to my dear friend, **Mara,** who oversaw the production of my Reiki books and DVDs and without whom this probably would never have been published.

ABOUT THE AUTHOR

Gail Thackray was raised in Yorkshire, England and prides herself on having kept her English down-to-earth sensibility. Her life changed at age forty when she discovered she was a medium and able to talk to spirits on the other side. Gail attributes her opening to the psychic world to her first Reiki attunement. Helping others connect to Source and to develop their own natural healing and psychic abilities is her passion. Gail lectures at events worldwide, doing live appearances as a healer, medium, and educator. When at home in Los Angeles, she writes, lectures, and teaches about mediumship, Reiki, animal communication, manifesting, and other aspects of spirituality.

Reiki Certification Manuals by Gail Thackray:

Reiki Level I – Energy Healing for Beginners

Reiki Level II – Practitioner Level Energy Healing

Reiki Level III/ART – Advanced Practitioner Level Energy Healing

Reiki Master – Master/Teacher Level Energy Healing

Reiki DVDs by Gail Thackray:

Reiki Level I – Workshop and attunement DVD

Reiki Level II – Workshop and attunement DVD

Reiki Level III/ART – Workshop and attunement DVD

Reiki Master – Workshop and attunement DVD

To order or for information on Gail's books, CDs, and DVDs on Reiki, energy healing, and other spiritual subjects, please go to:

www.GailThackray.com

REIKI NOTES

It is nice to keep notes of what you felt or experienced during your Reiki sessions.

_____

_____

_____

_____

_____

_____

_____

_____

_____

_____

_____

_____

_____

_____

_____

_____

CPSIA information can be obtained at www.ICGtesting.com
Printed in the USA
LVOW09s0111270116

472036LV00020B/573/P